Fear and Loathing:
Voting in America in 2016

*an Anti-Partisan Apathy to Action Approach
to Taking Back the Vote and Banking on Kids*

By: Lou Garino
Anti-Partisan American

Fear and Loathing: Voting in America in 2016
an Anti-Partisan Apathy to Action Approach by Lou Garino

Fear and Loathing: Voting in America in 2016,
an Anti-Partisan Apathy to Action Approach to Talking
Back the Vote and Banking on Kids.

ISBN 10: 1523933461
ISBN 13: 9781523933464

Printed independently in USA.

Sign up for free voting resources at LouGarino.com

Fear and Loathing: Voting in America in 2016
an Anti-Partisan Apathy to Action Approach by Lou Garino

Table of Contents

Sign up for free voting resources at LouGarino.com

Fear and Loathing: Voting in America in 2016
an Anti-Partisan Apathy to Action Approach by Lou Garino

Chapter 1 – Introduction

Voter Inspiration

The woman in labor who insisted on voting on the way to the hospital.

Illinois resident Galicia Malone did not let a little thing like being in labor stop her from casting her vote on Tuesday, Nov. 6, 2012.

Malone's contractions were already 5 minutes apart, and her water had already broken, but the 21-year-old new mother felt so strongly about making her voice heard that she powered through hard labor in order to fill out her ballot.

Fear and Loathing: Voting in America in 2016
an Anti-Partisan Apathy to Action Approach by Lou Garino

TRY BEING

INFORMED

INSTEAD OF JUST

OPINIONATED

Sign up for free voting resources at LouGarino.com

Fear and Loathing: Voting in America in 2016
an Anti-Partisan Apathy to Action Approach by Lou Garino

Democracy is a participatory sport and fewer people are participating than ever before. The effect??? Really, do I need to tell you? No, I think not. You are living with the results of voting apathy. Ask the folks in small towns and big cities across America whose government is out of touch with the needs of its citizens. These citizens have been forgotten by their politicians and their government, and their community suffers devastating effects as a result of a pathetic voting turnout. Why do the people with the most to lose so often choose not to participate in their own governance? We're a polarized nation on many, many levels, being currently ran by a broken two party system that is more content in pissing on each other's leg than, you know, actually governing. Thousands of towns across America have fallen into the huge hole of disconnect that voting apathy has dug. Unfortunately, voter apathy is running across the nation at lightning speed, like an epidemic attacking free society, free thought, and free choice. Poll numbers are down everywhere, as less people are participating, and less people debating; however, the worst is that less people are caring. The stakes have never been higher, and we are on the cusp of major decisions that will shape the future of our nation and the planet forever. From immigration reform, and

Fear and Loathing: Voting in America in 2016
an Anti-Partisan Apathy to Action Approach by Lou Garino

threat of global war, to the loss of liberties in the name of safety, there are some major chips on the table that need to be played. Our country needs help now if we are going to turn this condition around! Voting relationships begin at home, along with the local government and the peoples' interaction with it. The time is now to begin filling the gap of disconnect between our citizens and our government. Abraham Lincoln said, "The philosophy in the classroom today will be the philosophy of the government in one generation." God, I hope he's right, and we can bank on kids to pull this democracy out of our downward spiral.

With so much at stake, with so many things on the line, what are we choosing to do? We the people are choosing not to choose of course!! That's right... 90,000,000 eligible voters skipped the 2012 presidential election. We are bombarded with enormous numbers all day, but think about it... 90,000,000 people, more than the total population of California, Texas, and Florida combined, decided not to participate in the future governance of our country. In the Mid-Term election in 2014, for whatever reason, over 63% of eligible voters did not vote. In primary elections, where in most parts of the country the election actually decides the race because of strong party affiliation, the numbers are even far worse. Today in America, voter apathy runs as deep as the Continental Shelf. Voters are polarized after being beaten senseless from both sides, and the prospects of an engaged electorate is growing dimmer with each passing election cycle.

This book is going to explore just how we reached this point of the apathetical voter, and how this voter apathy affects towns and cities all over our nation. Just like a plane crash, the cause is never just one thing, but rather a combination of several factors. In towns and cities across America, the rot of disconnect between government, police and society has developed over the years. With each election cycle, people lose more of the very community they reside in when they don't vote. When people are not voting and not electing representation from within, conditions develop which can be potentially aggravated in the case of a bad event. In these conditions, one horrible event or accident, ignites a long filling powder keg. There are powder kegs building throughout our nation. The police department, the community, and the government are disconnected everywhere in our nation. As tragic as these events are, they could now become a beacon that shines a light for people to get involved and start taking back their government.

This book will take a hard look at the Presidential politicians that came down the pike over the last half century, and what they did and/or didn't do to put us where we are today. With each new election cycle comes a new crop of candidates, eager to tell you how different they are, who's to blame for the mess, and how much better things will be when they are in office. Okay then, we'll see how the voters in the nation were feeling before and after they were elected. Fair enough?? This would be fun I thought, actually it was painful.

The two political parties shall both feel our wrath when it comes to dishing out blame for the growing voter apathy epidemic. They both have had it far too good for far too long. Question: Is it easier to beat one opponent or two or five or?? How much easier is it to control your message if you only have one objecting opinion instead of five or six? You get my point. It seems we are living in a world of stifled debate instead of open and free debate, and we must change that. Without outside debate and outside candidates, nothing important will ever change.

More people believe in U.F.O.s than have faith in our government. If the two parties in America were accomplishing great results, we would not be having this discussion.

We, as members of the voting block in the United States of America, need to ALL look in the mirror. It is our personal decision to make, quite simply, we each have the power of choice. When one person speaks for ten, 12 or even 20 others in an election, things will fall and they will fall fast. If we want government by the people, we the people need to get off our ass and make it happen. We need to know who is representing us, and what they stand for and above all, hold them accountable!

With less people voting, why are there more laws being passed that make it even harder to vote than ever before? It is a trend that every citizen should be furious about. The right to vote is the most sacred thing we hold in America. With less and less people participating or even caring about elections, state after state are passing laws restricting voter

Sign up for free voting resources at LouGarino.com

access. Less advantaged towns are especially being hard hit by poll closings, limited early voting, I.D. laws, etc. We're going to look at this and other restrictions that are adding to the apathy of voters all over America.

The greatest thing about America is that its history proves that things can and do change, and that change can happen fast when the two parties refuse to address real issues. The growing abolitionist movement in the late 1840's was neither addressed by the Whigs nor the Democrats. Within ten years, the Republican Party controlled both houses and won the White House with Lincoln in 1860. We're going to look at all the ways we can take back our nation. We can take back our nation from the inter-global industrialists and international corrupt banking system. It comes down to one vote at a time; the power of one. America can fight the one tenth of one percent like George Soros and the Koch brothers. They dump billions of dollars in every election, slanting it in their interest and certainly not ours. Americans, like you and I, can battle them and WIN with awareness, common sense, a little pride, and action at the polls. The time is now, we can't

Sign up for free voting resources at LouGarino.com

afford the delay, and we can't afford to let another town in our great nation slip into indifference.

This book is not partisan, in fact, it's "Anti-Partisan." I'm mad as hell at both of them. Like many Americans, I have been continually let down by both parties, so I am NOT red or blue: I am Red, White and Blue. You will find a lot of new information in this book, some things I talk about are almost unreal, and I raise serious questions about major events that require a harder look. It will be up to you, my informed reader to further pursue the truth. If you tell people a big lie and keep repeating it they will eventually buy it, no matter how crazy it is. You will see how there is a thread of deception on an epic scale that both parties have come to endorse. The 1% would love nothing more than to have the 99% fight amongst each other while they get away with murder, which they are. If we continue to allow ourselves to be divided against each other while we're all getting screwed over, we're in deep trouble. The time has come for the people of this nation to unite and put the issues first and not the parties. Period.

The United States of America is on the verge of having its citizens lose total trust in the system. We allow people that we elect to fail us and lead us in a path WE don't want to go down. I know a whole lot of people on both sides but I don't know one, NOT ONE who thinks we should have one in five children, 14.1 million kids, living in poverty in America while we're spending one and a half trillion dollars on a new plane F-35 that is 69% over budget and basically not much better than what we have now. Plus, China has stolen the plans and has one just like it! According to Marian Edelman, the money spent on that plane alone could reduce childhood poverty by 60% for nineteen years, perhaps breaking free from intergenerational poverty. Our nation feels like it's on a train we can't control or stop. Our collectiveness feels hopeless and that our future is out of our hands. It's time we got courageous and acted like Americans. This nation must be of the people, by the people and for the people or it shall perish from this earth.

I have come to the conclusion that our best course of action is to learn as much as we can about our history and the FACTS about what IS going on. We as a nation need to care more about horrific Trade deals like the Trans Pacific Partnership than Bruce Jenner changing sexes. It IS time for critical thinking. Then we must participate, we must act, we

Sign up for free voting resources at LouGarino.com

must discuss and make aware the problems that face us. We need to have reasonable dialogue with each other. Above all, we need to teach all the children the responsibility of being a citizen of this great nation. I briefly touch on many subjects that could easily deserve volumes of books written about them, but this is written in an effort to begin your awareness. Feel free to explore all information to the end. Our children NEED to learn two fundamental building blocks of the American dream: 1) How to be an engaged, informed citizen and use that power voting in each election from the time you're 18 until you go to the big polling place in the sky; 2) How to have fiscal responsibility and take back the fiscal crisis in our country one student, one citizen at a time.

Along with being a Voting Advocate and Business Talk Show Host, I am the National Account Director of Banking On Kids. Banking On Kids is a fantastic program started 19 years ago and has been successful teaching young students the value of fiscal responsibility. It is a K-8 bank and curriculum where sponsoring banks set up real saving accounts in student run banks right in their own elementary school. Kids learn about saving, interest, compound interest and the banking system. If you would like to nominate a bank or for more information, go to LouGarino.com.

If we're going to take back our country we need to prepare and equip our youth to carry the torch of freedom for all, not just the few. That's why I'm awakening the electorate and "Banking On Kids."

Chapter 2 - Half Century Rundown

Voter Inspiration

The man who died and came back to vote.

In Detroit, Michigan, an elderly couple was filling out an absentee ballot on Monday when the man suddenly died.

A bystander sitting nearby performed CPR on the man until he finally revived several minutes later.

His first questions upon waking up? "Did I vote?"

The elderly man then sat up and finished filling out his ballot, telling his wife he only came back to do two things, to tell her that I love you and that I finished what I came here to do… vote."

THERE'S NO DIFFERENCE BETWEEN THE CANDIDATES, ANYWAY

Sign up for free voting resources at LouGarino.com

Fear and Loathing: Voting in America in 2016
an Anti-Partisan Apathy to Action Approach by Lou Garino

Candidates...ah...politicians. Can't live with 'em... well you know. Believe it or not, there was a time not long ago when people actually believed their government, really! No seriously. I mean it now... Post War America and the 50's found a government cruising through the post war boom, building interstates, and schools and for all intents and purposes doing an overall great job. Everyone trusted and liked Ike and our country basked in freedoms and patriotism, all the while knowing their country was working for them. All was good.... or so it seemed.

This chapter will be a brief rundown of the candidates and makes an attempt to reveal how the American voter was feeling at the time. As our nation evolved, it seemed our leaders did not. We face many of the same problems today as 50 years ago.

In the 1960 presidential election cycle, John F. Kennedy won the presidency by the narrowest of margins. 63% of eligible voters participated. The future of voter participation looked even better with all the educated boomers hitting the voting block soon. 60% of all American households watched the debates. Families often talked politics, not with disdain, but with hope and cause; real debate.

Congressmen actually represented their constituents and worked together to pass among other laws: The Voter Rights Act, the Equal Rights Amendment, Fair Housing, and numerous other social programs, including Medicare. Kennedy immediately united the country, and in 1961 he put down a challenge to put a man on the moon and return him safely to Earth. We did it by the end of the decade, at least that's what we were told.

But Kennedy never saw that moment, his dream and the dreams many others ended in Dallas, Texas on a warm November day when an assassin(s)? killed him. In as surreal of a moment as has ever existed in our nation's history, Lyndon Baines Johnson was sworn in as president on Air Force One as the widow Kennedy looked on with her bloodstained pink dress. The look on Jackie's face will forever be an emblazed stain on the nation's soul. Camelot and the magic of it was gone before Air Force One left the Lone Star State. Our country was shaken hard on two levels. First, we lost a young charismatic President, and second, we lost a First Lady that we were in love with, and we felt like we lost our family that day.

Fear and Loathing: Voting in America in 2016
an Anti-Partisan Apathy to Action Approach by Lou Garino

80% of Americans do not believe the official Warren Report that Lee Harvey Oswald acted alone. Why? Because he did not. Here is an example of something I encourage you, the aware reader of this book, to look further into this and forthcoming issues that I will address. I suggest you go to YouTube and view what Jim Marrs and others have to say about the truth and what really went down in Dallas, who benefitted and how it's been covered up so good for so long. BEWARE: Once you go down the rabbit hole, your life will not be the same. You will not like what you find. Just like everything in life, it's so much easier to look the other way or keep your blinders on while the stack of crap piles up all around you. Forget voter apathy, that's life apathy! Your participation in reading this book will hopefully get you in the top 1%. The 1% of awareness in America!

As if on cue, immediately after Kennedy's death, the United States went from an advisory role in the Vietnam Conflict to having troops in country. The false flag operation in the Gulf of Tonkin (This event was staged to get us into the conflict, later admitted by the Government.) quickly gave power to Johnson to escalate the conflict in Vietnam. If Kennedy had lived there was no way he was getting suckered into

Sign up for free voting resources at LouGarino.com

Fear and Loathing: Voting in America in 2016
an Anti-Partisan Apathy to Action Approach by Lou Garino

Vietnam, but Johnson fired up the war machine and the defense contractors got what they wanted. Big money was gaining more control in our government and they may have had a hand in forming it. But the situation with Johnson and the conflict in Vietnam had surprisingly little buzz going into the '64 election.

Johnson easily won in 1964 largely behind the Kennedy momentum. The country was in no mood to change captains again so soon. The Vietnam Conflict was not yet rancid and things looked pretty good going forward. It's hard to believe the remainder of the decade would be among the most tumultuous times in our nation's history. The fleeting sense of unity in the early 1960's quickly gave way to the ever escalating conflict in Vietnam and our nation was forced to choose sides. As our commitment to the war grew and the body count climbed, our country began to splinter. The educated boomers that were entering the voting block in masses were not following in line with the old guard. They were using the education their parents proudly gave them to question authority, something their parents never did and seldom had to do. Politics quickly became us vs. them...war vs. anti-war. Human issues were being forced out of their dark closet and laid upon the table for a long overdue decision. It's time for Equal Rights! But not for some. Another deep issue, another fraction. Our country was quickly awakened from a deep sleep and was groggy with change. The assassinations, segregation, equal voting, war, riots in our cities.... the status quo hadn't been shaken like that for 100 years since the Civil War. It was a lot and the emotions of the country showed, overflowing on a Sunday in Selma, Alabama when hatred and its evil cousin bigotry was on display for the world to see. Was this the "Light Bulb" moment? Perhaps now we can reason again? And after 100 years of voting silence, perhaps these newly freed voters will breathe new life in the heart of democracy? Perhaps.

The '68 election was the beginning of the great divide. Johnson, well, he had enough; he "would not seek nor would he accept the nomination of his party to be president." The lies, the war and maybe even his conscience buckled LBJ, so he loaded up the truck and went back to the ranch in the Texas hill country. I met Lyndon's first cousin, Ava Johnson Cox, in Johnson City, Texas in 1986. She was a salt of the earth woman who surprisingly did not dote on the cousin she grew up with. If fact, I closed a business transaction on a table where four presidents of the

Fear and Loathing: Voting in America in 2016
an Anti-Partisan Apathy to Action Approach by Lou Garino

United States had eaten dinner, and I can't remember her saying one good thing about her little cousin.

America saw his V.P., Hubert Humphries, as a continuum of Lyndon. Richard M. Nixon was just tricky enough to win the hearts of the nation and the White House. Reading the 1968 Republican Party's platform now looks like a page from the modern day Democrat playbook. I welcome anyone to read it and see how far our country has moved. As equal rights passed, the country further separated. Old world hatred and segregation were holding on in '68 with Governor George Wallace of Alabama running for American Independent party, receiving over 9,000,000 votes and winning five southern states and over 13% of the vote. Voters were now starting to feel weary as both Vietnam and unrest in the streets escalated.

The '70s rolled in and Vietnam rolled on, but the country stuck with Nixon. Nixon was tricky and he had the big money, big bank, and big PR machine behind him. The '72 election was a total landslide for Nixon. McGovern was painted as a left wing extremist and the nation got behind Nixon. Dick, however, got caught in his little scandal at the Watergate Hotel...

Fear and Loathing: Voting in America in 2016
an Anti-Partisan Apathy to Action Approach by Lou Garino

Dick says, "I'm not a crook" but ultimately he lied, was impeached and had to leave office in disgrace. His departure did for voter confidence what Fonz's shark jump did for Happy Days. Nothing hits the voter's heart more than having the guy you voted for and believed in thrown out of office.

Sworn into office after Nixon resigned was Gerald Ford, the first U.S. president never to have won a national office. Ford was an appointed V.P... Why was he appointed? Because Nixon's original Vice President, Spiro Agnew, was indicted on the good ole' politician trifecta; bribery, conspiracy, and tax fraud. Now Gerry is Commander-in-Chief, without ever receiving a vote for either capacity and then appointing a Rockefeller as his 2nd in Command. Just the perception of impropriety suggested by naming a headpiece for one of world's richest most powerful families is ridiculous, yet there it is. Now we have a President and a Vice President that not one American was able to vote for. Not one person. At this moment our Presidential vote was devalued and to nil, and the former President and Vice President of the United States of America left office in disgrace. Voter confidence?? They can't even finish their term in office.

Sign up for free voting resources at LouGarino.com

Fear and Loathing: Voting in America in 2016
an Anti-Partisan Apathy to Action Approach by Lou Garino

With the fall of Saigon, a terrible economy, and the fact that Ford pardoned Nixon, America was not happy. America needed an outsider, and straight from the peanut fields came Jimmie "The Lamb" Carter, a soft spoken southern governor. He polled at 1% when he announced his candidacy, so he literally came out of the peanut field. It seemed Jimmy just couldn't get it going and "Billy Beer" just wasn't catching Budweiser. A stagnant economy, gas lines, and the hostage crisis doomed any good he may have tried to do. Voters wanted a solid guy and he was, but his wheels never caught traction they just spun in the mud.

Then came the Dutch....Like a knight riding in from a Hollywood B-movie set, preaching God, Family, and Country came Ronald Reagan. Reagan did unite the county and took the '80 election in a landslide. He spent more on defense than any two before him and it did end the cold war. The fall of the Berlin wall was a great moment in world history, and we the voters were taking pride in our nation again. But the trickle down policies he instituted are still being felt by the ever decreasing middle class. The huge income gap alone is enough to cause voter apathy. Apathetic in and of itself. If people think we will always be run by the rich and there is nothing you can do about it, including voting, we're in trouble.

H.W. Bush was the last of the greatest generation to lead this nation and took Dukakis in '88, but his kinder, gentler nation could not inspire like Reagan before him. He freed Kuwait, claimed the oil for his Skull and Crossbones friends, but didn't finish Hussain. His Old School ways were becoming outdated, out of touch, and his message was putting the voters to sleep.

No worries, in '92 we were introduced to William Jefferson Clinton and his band of Arkansas misfits. He entered the race like someone wearing a pink tuxedo to their prom. No matter how hard he tried, he just couldn't blow the '92 election. Both his youth and enthusiasm were contagious to the boomers from which he came. Timing was right and the new tech driven economy rocked in the '90s and drove to a re-election over Bob Dole. However, Ross Perot fired up the electorate and made the two parties actually have to deal with the deficit and other issues that they had passed over for too long. While the economy grew, so did people's loathing for Willie's slickness. Voting perception and participation seldom increases when the leader of the free world can't keep his rocket in his pocket.

From the bowels of Texas and the remedial classes at Yale, came the W... George Walker Bush. Fresh off a stolen election, his limo was pelted with rocks during his inauguration. To the voter, there is nothing like the feeling that your vote doesn't count, especially if it doesn't. Thousands of votes, discarded because the punch hole did not fully separate from the voting card. It was a nightmare. The hanging chad!!! Remember that? Goodness! Dubya inherited a beautiful house of a nation, with friendly neighbors and money in the bank. In eight short years, he spent all the money, mortgaged the house to the teeth, and pissed off every neighbor we had on the planet. For his swan song he made sure he covered his Wall Street cronies' greedy mistakes with a lil ole Trillion Dollar Bailout. Makes me feel warm and fuzzy...how about you? The country now totally divided, as more and more apathy ensues, but if only we had hope.

Enter stage right, Barack Obama who easily defeated John McCain. Voters were excited, grassroots movements ran wild, voter registration grew, and the people voted for change. But nothing

Sign up for free voting resources at LouGarino.com

changed. It's like we keep ordering at the same restaurant and we get the wrong food every time. When you fire people up and they vote for change, and then nothing happens, there's going to be a huge letdown. It could mean permanent disillusionment for the newest round of voters. America was sold a false bill of goods with Obama. He has done more to hurt on civil liberties, hurt labor, help Wall Street, and keep the war machine going than anyone thought possible.

Given the choice between nothing getting done, or nothing changing and Mitt Romney, America chose "nothing getting done." The 1950's white-starched boardroom looking guy is just too tight, especially when he made his billions taking over cash fat companies, destroying their pension funds and moving them overseas. It shows that people are voting less for what a candidate believes and more against the alternative. There we have it, my 50+ year stroll down Apple Pie Lane. As we see, apathy begets apathy, one poor cycle after the next, STUFF stacks up and now our country hasn't been this divided on this many levels ever. Divide us they do. Why? The truth, like many BIG truths today, is hidden right in front of our eyes. Of course, it makes us easier to control. Who's paying? We are of course. Are you feeling the growing disconnect? Yeah, me too, and I don't like it at all.

The thread of leadership over the last half century has certainly given credence to the state of our voting consciousness, or lack thereof, in both obvious and underlying ways. The quality of the candidates we just discussed are just a small example of the quality of all elected officials throughout the United States. Dare I say that the apathy of voters mirrors the quality of candidates? Four of the last seven governors from Illinois were sent to prison. 89% of the people living there believe their state government is corrupt. If this book was about government corruption it would never get finished. It's a small wonder that when given a choice, voters are choosing not to choose.

Just look at our last crop of our hard working members of Congress, shall we? The 113th edition, or as I like to call them, the "Fighting 113th". Out of the 112 previous editions of Congress that the voters of our nation sent to Washington to represent them, our boys and girls, the Fighting 113th, well, they finished last. LAST! The least productive Congress in our history. A whopping 15% approval rating which really only points out that 15% of the people are truly freakin' nuts if they had any approval whatsoever for the ridiculous performances being laid out on a daily basis by our elected officials. Pass the Civil Rights Bill??? Shoot, if this Congress had a kidney stone, they would not pass it.

As Americans, we need to overcome poor candidates and elected officials by remembering they're all temporary. We need to remember they work for us; we don't work for them. They are as temporary in Washington as they are in any corner of America.

We need to recruit better and better candidates from outside the box, business people from outside of Washington, anyone that's outside the pockets of big corporations and Wall Street. Someone that isn't ordained from the Global Elites but from the people. You really only need three things to change a democracy: unity, hope, and action.

Page 32

Chapter 3 - Voting Laws

Fear and Loathing: Voting in America in 2016
an Anti-Partisan Apathy to Action Approach by Lou Garino

Voter Inspiration

The hurricane victims who didn't let a lack of electricity keep them from voting. In the wake of the devastating super-storm Hurricane Sandy, over a million homes and businesses were still without power on Election Day in New York and New Jersey.

Many polling stations were among the damaged buildings, and gas shortages and a lack of electricity made getting to the polls difficult for thousands of people.

The governors of both states invoked extraordinary measures to help voters participate in the election. People were allowed to submit their votes by fax or email in some places, and others were given substitute ballots at any polling station they could get to, instead of having to find their specific station. In some places, voters waited in long lines to vote in the generator-fueled tents.

Sign up for free voting resources at LouGarino.com

Fear and Loathing: Voting in America in 2016
an Anti-Partisan Apathy to Action Approach by Lou Garino

VOTE FOR NOBODY

NOBODY WILL KEEP ELECTION PROMISES

NOBODY WILL LISTEN TO YOUR CONCERNS

NOBODY WILL HELP THE POOR & UNEMPLOYED

NOBODY CARES!

IF NOBODY IS ELECTED, THINGS WILL BE

BETTER

FOR EVERYONE

NOBODY TELLS THE TRUTH

Fear and Loathing: Voting in America in 2016
an Anti-Partisan Apathy to Action Approach by Lou Garino

Our country's Constitution includes the words: government of the people, by the people, and for the people. Suffrage is part of "by the people," in fact that's exactly what it is. The Constitution also gives the power to hold and monitor elections to the states. Each state has its very own voting laws and voting methods. Some states hold separate primaries, while others have both parties simultaneously on the ballot. Some have early voting, some don't. Some have I.D laws, some don't. Some have different ways you can vote within their own state! If I was going to write about how crazy elections are across the country, I could get a mini-series. No joke!

The "by the people" in our country has pretty much been whoever the government wanted it to be. In our countries birth, voters were designated only to white male landowners and other white male tax payers. It was pretty much that way across the states, and by the Civil War it went on to include all white males. So our democracy was always based on voter seclusion. When I hear people talk as if Voter Exclusion is a new thing, makes me laugh. Our country was built on closed elections. Closed to all but white males.

Fear and Loathing: Voting in America in 2016
an Anti-Partisan Apathy to Action Approach by Lou Garino

Voters in the post-Civil War saw our nation move achingly slow toward more voting freedoms. Four of the post-Civil War constitutional amendments were in regards to voting. The 14th amendment giving equal citizenship was a start in the right direction. It looked good on paper but did little to change elections and voting in America, especially in the southern states. Jim Crowe laws in state after state were designed for keeping blacks from voting. Let's not forget violence! Poll taxes, religious tests, literacy tests and many other ridiculous state by state laws all served to dissolution the minority and the poor voters. By 1902, all 11 confederate states had a poll tax. Minority voters across most of the country basically were put to sleep for a hundred years and in many ways they are still paying the price of achieving voter equality. Towns across America, like Ferguson, Missouri for example (Pop. 40,000) are still paying the price. In the 2013 local elections in Ferguson there was a 6% voter turnout. Without participation in the election of their very government in their own backyard, their local representation looks something like this: 50 out of 53 police officers are white, all school board members are white, and all but one council person is white. Doesn't sound like "of the people" to me because the "by the people" don't show up to vote.

Sign up for free voting resources at LouGarino.com

Fear and Loathing: Voting in America in 2016
an Anti-Partisan Apathy to Action Approach by Lou Garino

This is NOT about color, but about how quickly your own back yard could look so different so fast if one person votes for 20.

At last the power of woman's suffrage movement that began in 1840 was unleashed in 1920 with the 19th Amendment giving women full voting rights. There were a handful of states that gave them the right to vote earlier but now it was across America. The political landscape never changed so much at one time ever. It was the political awakening of a sleeping giant that the status quo be aware. The '20s roared with change and voter outlook was on the rise until the stock market crashed in 1929, driving America and the world into the great depression. All the momentum that was built in the '20s was now into a long and painful sleep. People were beat down, prospects were bleak and apathy was everywhere. Everyone was just trying to survive and get through the day. We had Franklin D. Roosevelt and that was enough for the voters. The New Deal was their mantra.

America's coma ended on December 7, 1941. The Japanese attack on Pearl Harbor ignited the United States in a way never before seen. The entire country rallied around a cause, THE cause, a fight we simply could not lose. America and its voters picked F.D.R an unprecedented four times and the torch went to Give 'Em Hell Harry Truman when Roosevelt passed. The voters trusted Harry and then liked Ike, Dwight Eisenhower, a former general in the war and leader of the Allied Command. While the woman electorate was engaging in the voting process, large blocks of minority voters were not even yet on the radar. Forces at the time did not want total participation, and there are the same forces working within our country now. Even after WWII, very few things changed in regards to our voting trends. Small rural black America was locked out of the voting process and inner city was just as bad. 1000s of small urban towns that were still predominantly white right after the war changed as the urbanization of America began. White people moved to the suburbs and minorities moved in. Now at this time you have whole towns that either have Jim Crowe laws or other prohibitive steps to vote. The children suffer from this lack of a voting culture. They grow up to not engage but accept. Most people learn to vote from their parents or family, what happens when you never knew anyone that voted?

Sign up for free voting resources at LouGarino.com

Fear and Loathing: Voting in America in 2016
an Anti-Partisan Apathy to Action Approach by Lou Garino

Can you imagine growing up in an environment where no one ever voted? Not your mother, not your father your uncle or friends have ever voted. It's a frightening thought to many Americans but a sad fact for many more. One of the great things about America is that each generation carries the torches of the generation before them. But what if you were never handed the torch of choice? You never miss what you never have, and a culture that doesn't vote becomes the generationally disengaged. What transpires from this is a sad loss of a moral compass.

In 1960, a long overdue issue was forced from darkness and into the light. In 1965, The Voting Rights Act, the 24th amendment to the Constitution was ratified to give the federal government more power over state elections, ending poll taxes and other voting restrictive measures. Hundreds of years of bigotry does not go away easily. The people organizing registration drives were met with resistance, hate and even death. States continued to intimidate voters and repress on all fronts the efforts being made engage voters. On March 7, 1965, 600 innocent men, women and children protesting for voting registration were beaten by police in riot gear, with billy clubs, dosed with high powered fire hoses, and attacked by police dogs. 60 people were hospitalized. This debacle known as Bloody Sunday in Selma, Alabama was on display for all the world to see. The shame of that moment as an American is still being felt. It was 50 short years ago but long enough that today's voters don't realize the struggle it was to be freely able to vote. I assure you that every one of those people that marched in Selma that day never missed an election. They know the price of freedom and they will never let it go.

The 1960s were tumultuous times for voting. Voices everywhere wanted to be heard and change does not come easily, especially in the governance of a nation. The younger block of potential voters wanted their voices heard. Our nation was gripped in bowels of Vietnam and our young men and woman were dying in the field, young poor kids from towns all over America. There was a united cry from among them... Old enough to die for our country but not old enough to vote. Good Point! If the government wanted these boys to keep showing up to die when they were drafted, they better appease them a little. In 1968, the 26th amendment gave 18 year olds the right to vote.

Fear and Loathing: Voting in America in 2016
an Anti-Partisan Apathy to Action Approach by Lou Garino

The laws.... With all these newly freed voters there was a good feeling among the electorate that things were about to change. We got through the '60s and we're still here. The feeling in the country was change. As the boomers were now adults, their beliefs and morays becoming more the fabric of a new society and way of thinking. Change was felt to be possible and the '72 election brought excitement to the new block of voters. Registration drives were on campuses nationwide, in southern churches and across America. Most of the new voters wanted an end to Vietnam and the choice for them was clear: it would be George McGovern for president, while the old guard was taking Nixon. It was a landslide for Nixon. The new block of voters were mostly disappointed but certainly not disillusioned. Their strong disdain for Nixon didn't stop with the election and neither would their voting.

Then came Watergate. The Nixon resignation cut through the heart of voters on both sides. A humiliation to all the millions that put him in office, and I told you so from the millions that opposed him. Voters were now feeling let down and who could blame them? Nixon going down in flames is one thing, but losing faith in the office of the presidency is

Sign up for free voting resources at LouGarino.com

another. The new larger sail of the American electorate had just had the wind die out.

The voter laws that were passed in the '60s were slow to be enforced. Federal over sight laws (designed to protect voter rights) progress was being made. Campaigns and registration drives were happening with each election cycle. Laws were on the books and everything seemed like our nations voting worries would soon be worked out.

The next two decades with the 1980s and the 1990s brought a semblance of stability to voting across America. While voter apathy was high, there was at least a chance to cast your ballot without compromise.

Then came the election of 2000. A fiasco to say the least. The outcome was ultimately decided by the Supreme Court in what was THE craziest election in U.S. history. Voters around America were livid that this election was decided in the court system and not the polls. Political operatives were in Florida, turning everything upside down until the required results were achieved.

Sign up for free voting resources at LouGarino.com

Fear and Loathing: Voting in America in 2016
an Anti-Partisan Apathy to Action Approach by Lou Garino

Parties, one in particular, realized they could change results of elections by tweaking the rules and boundaries of districts. The voting landscape was now back to exclusion once again as the theme. This was all done in a very subtle way with programs like redistricting, new I.D. Laws, less early voting, less polls, inaccessible polls, longer lines, you name it. It's like a bunch of bullies stand in front of the door but won't let you in.

"This is almost unprecedented," said Lawrence Norden, deputy director of the Brennan Center's Democracy Program, which tracks voting laws and which published the analysis. "We have not seen this number of restrictive voting laws pass probably since the end of the 20th century. Certainly, this is the biggest rollback since the civil-rights era in terms of voting rights."

According to the Brennan Center's analysis:

• Five of the 10 states with the highest black turnout in 2008 have passed restrictive voting laws.

Sign up for free voting resources at LouGarino.com

Fear and Loathing: Voting in America in 2016
an Anti-Partisan Apathy to Action Approach by Lou Garino

• Seven of the 12 states that have seen the biggest growth in the Latino population in the last decade have passed restrictive voting laws.

Most of the new laws were established ostensibly to curb voter fraud, which analysts say is rare.

We, the people are getting smacked upside our head with regards to our voting rights, especially among our poor. It's hard enough as it is to get citizens to vote, the last thing we want as a nation is to make it harder. No one knows what their towns need more than the residents. Citizens need to make the choice and bring in their own leaders that affect their lives every day, whether it's the school board, the council or Mayor. We are being played as if our state government can use us as pawns in their political chess game. It's sickening. Parties are taking advantage of state legislators to pass these restrictive laws. How evil is that?!

Since 2011, 41 states have introduced restrictive voter legislation. Why on earth would 41 states want to repress voter turnout? They have passed laws restricting voter access by overall, 25 laws and two executive actions passed in 19 states that have restricted voter access. Those are the ones that didn't get blocked by the court system. Some states are even defying court orders to implement their new laws. What the hell is going on, people?

Herein lies the apathy. The soundbites from politicians tell us they want fair voting yet their actions seem to say differently. Just like all issues, we need to know where our candidates stand on equal voting regardless of party. In fact, most detrimental voting laws are enacted where minorities are growing in Republican held districts. The Republicans or any other party need to adjust to the will of the people NOT keep them from voting. Our dialogue must begin at the inception of every candidate's entry into the arena. How do you feel about repressive voting laws? Electronic Ballots (Evil)? How do you feel about term limits? Obviously, that's a tough question for incumbents. You get it, it starts with open dialogue not sound bites.

If all are not free to vote, then no one is free. One person, one vote. It's really that simple. We must demand a fair, consistent and honest way to for us as a nation to vote; otherwise our vote or our republic won't really matter anymore.

Sign up for free voting resources at LouGarino.com

Chapter 4 – Parties

Fear and Loathing: Voting in America in 2016
an Anti-Partisan Apathy to Action Approach by Lou Garino

Voter Inspiration

The famous rapper who paid people to vote.

Rapper, The Game, wanted to help victims of Hurricane Sandy in New York get to the polls.

TMZ reports that the celebrity donated $10,000 to about 500 voters who had been stranded by the storm.

The money was intended to help voters who were affected by the storm pay for gas or transportation to get them to the polling stations. In fact, he even used his own car to shuttle people to and from the polls.

Sign up for free voting resources at LouGarino.com

Fear and Loathing: Voting in America in 2016
an Anti-Partisan Apathy to Action Approach by Lou Garino

LOUGARINO.COM

Sign up for free voting resources at LouGarino.com

Fear and Loathing: Voting in America in 2016
an Anti-Partisan Apathy to Action Approach by Lou Garino

How is the two party system working to answer our nation's real problems in a timely and diligent manner? How is it serving the citizens of our nation? How is it serving themselves? How is it serving the corporations of our nation? We see the slow dismantlement of small urban towns and cities across our country. Detroit looks like a demilitarized zone. Towns are falling like dominos all over, all the time, and it's not a red or a blue thing, again, it's a red, white and blue thing. Walmart continues to wipe out small businesses in every small town they enter, getting extremely fat all the while increasing our huge trade deficit to China and paying such a low wage that you and I as tax payers supplement their workers 6.2 billion dollars a year. There are small towns in Alabama that vote consistently red which are hurting every bit as much as small towns like Ferguson that vote strictly blue. Disconnection between the voter, or lack thereof, has no political affiliation: bad is bad, period. If either side had the answer, why don't we have it? What we do have is town after town going through long decay at the hands of both parties.

Sign up for free voting resources at LouGarino.com

Fear and Loathing: Voting in America in 2016
an Anti-Partisan Apathy to Action Approach by Lou Garino

The plurality of the two party system for choosing the elected officials of our government has settled in as the norm of American politics. There is nothing in the Constitution about political parties. In fact, many of the founding fathers opposed them vehemently. It was their strong views however that actually started parties in America. Alexander Hamilton wanted a strong federal government so the people that got behind him were called the Federalists. People against a strong federal government were of course the Anti-Federalists that later became the Democrat-Republicans.

Since there is no regard to political parties in the constitution why don't we have a multitude of political parties? How did it flow to really have just two parties? That's a fair enough question, isn't it? Well, there is no exact reason but it is believed that since the inception of our nation, most importantly issues debated, people found themselves on one side or the other. When people realized they felt the same way on many issues then they started aligning themselves together. Our system of government lent itself for a two party system to develop but it has morphed into a hierarchy of sorts with little difference in branding at all and that is a huge issue.

Sign up for free voting resources at LouGarino.com

Fear and Loathing: Voting in America in 2016
an Anti-Partisan Apathy to Action Approach by Lou Garino

Republican and Democrat are really just labels defining a conservative and a progressive agenda. It was the Democratic Party prior to the Civil War that was staunchly conservative, so much so that it sprung the new progressive Republican Party into power in the 1850s, and the presidency in 1860. Basically, there have always been a conservative and a progressive movement and for whatever reason most of America just got in line behind one of them.

The benefit of having only two parties from the party's standpoint is that you only have one opponent to defeat! Imagine in your business if you only had one competitor? Pretty sweet! They can get all their candidates, round 'em up, and put them under one big umbrella. Ever notice when most people are running for office they actually sound like individuals, and then once elected they start talking in soundbites? You start knowing what they're going to say before they say it. It's like they went to a secret chamber and were reconstructed like Body Snatchers and they all start talking alike, all bought and paid for by the same people. Proponents of the two party system say additional parties would not enable legislation to form a consensus in Congress and get enough votes to pass laws. How much is getting done

Sign up for free voting resources at LouGarino.com

Fear and Loathing: Voting in America in 2016
an Anti-Partisan Apathy to Action Approach by Lou Garino

now I ask? As we know, the fighting 113th Congress was the least effective in history.

At this juncture in American history, you are force fed that we essentially have only two choices. The media seems to want it that way. You never see a Libertarian or Green Party candidate on the presidential debate. Why not? What is their fear of more ideas and open dialogue from all sides? With only two choices, it just does not allow for different opinions and different issues. Besides, all the media makes you feel as if you're throwing your vote away by voting 3rd party. They want opinions stifled and everyone fitting neatly into a box. The problems we're confronted with in our own towns and nation are very complex. One size (their size) fits all cannot, and is not, working. It is also a cauldron for ideological extremism that takes us off the real battles that need to be fought. Hard line positions have overtaken reasonable debate, and even regular Americans have trouble openly talking about America because they themselves fall so deeply into one of these two parties. Do we forget we're all Americans? Since the Cold War ended, we don't have the Russians to hate anymore. Do we have to start hating ourselves? It certainly appears so and the parties are loving it!

Page 53

Fear and Loathing: Voting in America in 2016
an Anti-Partisan Apathy to Action Approach by Lou Garino

This is a point of contention because America IS divided and we truly have the Democrats and the Republicans to thank for that. As a voter, I am coming up on my 10th Presidential election cycle. I can say unequivocally that our nation is as divided now as it's been since Vietnam. We have entertainment shows posing as news outlets that stoke the flames of fear and hatred. Our news features what the Kardashians did this summer, while millions of gallons of nuclear waste pours out of Fukoshima, Japan every day. The real news is lost in the minutia or it's passed over altogether. Objective opinion is hard to find anywhere. People just don't have time to read print, internet or even newspapers or find other opinions on the matters of the day. It's just so much easier to fall in line and let someone else do the thinking for you, and fall into living in a reality of sound bites. News on TV is a psychological operation that's runs loop after loop until everything you see becomes a reality.

Since everyone is familiar with Ferguson, Missouri, I will use this as an example of how a town melts into oblivion with the help of their leaders. Because of long standing obstacles, citizens in Ferguson have a disproportionately high rental rate and very little civic participation and stake in the town's governance. The results are typical of an apathetic culture. Normandy School District that services Ferguson was one of three out of 500 school districts through the state of Missouri to lose their accreditation because of poor performance. Missouri law allows students of failed districts to transfer to higher-performing schools in the surrounding suburbs, but the failing school district has to pay tuition and transportation costs to get the kids to their new schools. The 1,000 transfer students of Normandy obviously had no desire to remain in the "new" failed district, but the cost was quite high, so, incredibly, the state board voted to waive accreditation of the collaborative rather than classify the new district as unaccredited. Ferguson's teenagers were therefore trapped in a failed school because state politicians didn't want to pay for them to transfer out. What if you had a child in this district? With this beginning in life they are more easily shackled into a world that from which they may never break free or care enough to about to change it by voting.

When people fall in line behind a party they are taken for granted. If a particular party wins in an area over and over and this area continually declines, it's

Page 55

the voter who loses. Many voters couldn't possibly identify with the other party and the quality of candidates they have had to choose from in their own party couldn't cut the mustard. Over the years the few people in these towns that did vote increasingly faded out because the results they received from their elected officials were unsatisfactory. All they had to do to see the failure was look on the street where they lived or the school their kids went to.

When only one out of 20 people vote in local elections, who's actually doing the electing? Small towns need to realize that a few thousand or even a few hundred votes can take an election and a few votes can make the difference. The line between apathy and integrity is not that wide. If folks in small towns actually started to vote they could easily have all new leadership in the next election cycle. A 20% turnout could turn the whole city government upside down. If towns can look within for a few good leaders and get people behind them, things could change lightning fast. Think of this for your town and how quickly things could change if people started thinking this way.

Fear and Loathing: Voting in America in 2016
an Anti-Partisan Apathy to Action Approach by Lou Garino

Does anyone remember when we got only three channels on the television? Seemed like plenty. It really wasn't all that long ago. We went from an agriculture driven society to a tech driven society in a few short generations. Simplicity has long been replaced with choice and information. Our society has changed faster than anyone could have ever imagined. Two choices just aren't enough for the American voter anymore. Even staunch Republicans and Democrats find their party is only serving part of what they want. What if I'm a social liberal and a fiscal conservative? What if you are a social conservative but also want healthcare for everyone? As time goes by, the relationships between people and their affiliated party grows weaker and weaker and the gap widens.

While they frantically fight each other at every seam, there really isn't much difference between the parties. Regardless of the will of the people they just go about their own way as if the only thing they have to do is get people to vote for them again. In 2008, America voted for change, they voted for the repeal of the Patriot Act, they voted for less NSA. They voted for healthcare and the revocation of the Bush tax cut on the top 1% in our country. Oh yeah, we wanted the crooks in Wall Street to own what they did to get the trillion-dollar bail out to save our collapsing economy, and those dang wars. There was an excitement in the air that change was coming and finally a new direction was about to begin to move forward.

Seven years later in 2015, the National Security Agency (NSA), AKA big brother, is on steroids spying on us citizens in the name of freedom...makes me sick! Makes everybody sick. We're accelerating the loss of our personal liberties faster than any time in our existence. The temporary Patriot Act is still moving right along, thank you, keeping all the liberty restrictive laws in in effect, I guess permanently. No one ever talks about it anymore, there's way too much other crap piling up faster than we can shovel. So much for temporary. To keep our government from total collapse by a threatened government shutdown, the Bush tax cuts were left to stay. Healthcare? Don't make me laugh. Because of the two party gridlock, we have a mish mosh of confusion not even close to something workable. Why do people without health insurance so bitterly oppose it? How can anyone that I elect say we can't insure our citizens but we can spend 51% of our budget on a military to expand our empire around the world? The health of citizens is in the hands of lawmakers. You feeling good about that? These guys couldn't pass anything let alone a worthwhile healthcare plan. The two parties... not only didn't they work together, they fought each other on every single point. How could two parties solve our humungous health care crisis without agreeing on one thing? Which one of those white collar billionaire Wall Street guys went to jail? Really can't think of any...and how about them wars. Glad we ended them. Oh, that's right, we're bombing as my fingers hit these keys!

So much for change even when we the people want it. I am not on a stump screaming for a third party; maybe I am, but it is quite apparent the two parties in power now are doing nothing at a time our nation needs real dialogue, real debate, and real solutions that people can get behind. The most important thing third and fourth party candidates may bring are new ideas confronting old problems. No one worried about the National Deficit until Ross Perot made it a valid point in the '92 debates. Imagine how far down the line on issues had they been argued in the presidential debate earlier...term limits for example, or legalization of medical marijuana,

Sign up for free voting resources at LouGarino.com

privatization of jails. There could be issue after issue that would need to be addressed once someone brings it to the debate. We need to demand our networks allow more candidates in the debates to openly discuss all issues, not just the ones the two parties want to discuss. The very last thing we all want are the networks deciding who gets to debate, really!? A candidate doesn't have a chance if not on that stage. If there is not a candidate in the debate that people align with, when people feel like no one represents them; so they stay home on Election Day, and they've been staying home a lot lately.

The plural party system has served our country pretty good for over 200 years. It has adjusted to the will of the people when the will of the people was strong enough to force change. Our nation's history has proven that parties come and go when people decide that any party is not serving them. Just because things are this way doesn't mean they'll stay this way. The red and the blue have each taken their base for granted for way too long. The less they do, the more frustrated everyone becomes. That opens up new roads for new candidates whether in the red or blue or in a new party all together.

Page 60

Sign up for free voting resources at LouGarino.com

Fear and Loathing: Voting in America in 2016
an Anti-Partisan Apathy to Action Approach by Lou Garino

Over time a new party could come into power and one of our current parties may be marginalized or cease to exist all together. The ebb and the flow of our electoral cycles is slowly turning society into have and have nots, with the have nots losing badly. The people not voting are the ones that that have the worst of the deal. Ferguson is the prime example of what happens when people feel outside of the system. You feel anyone of authority is lying to you and out to get you, somehow, someway; and you have really good proof of that. Well, people aren't going to vote under those circumstances and that's what we have right here right now!

The revolving door in Washington that goes on to serve special interests serves no one in America except big business. Our politicians are like our CEOs, with huge golden parachutes in the name of lobbying or corporate figurehead jobs. Eric Cantor lost in his state's primary and immediately resigned and took a 3.4 million dollar a year job to run a Wall Street investment firm. The Wall Street Journal reported the bank was using Cantor to compete for business. Do you think being the former House Majority Leader will help a little? Sickening to play on such a crooked field. The revolving door of Washington to Wall Street

Sign up for free voting resources at LouGarino.com

or lobbying for big pharma or defense contractors or 100s of other lobbying efforts disintegrates the fabric that the American voters need in order to feel that they can make a difference.

This is not a book of specifics or I can write all day just about lobbying in America. I can write for a month on corruption and probably a year if I really wanted. What I'm trying to do is to lay out a reason of how we got here without going off on hundreds of tangents to rant about in our political process. We didn't get here overnight. It has been a culmination of many different factors over the years. Our parties morphed into what many people see as one party with two names.

A new Rasmussen Reports national telephone survey finds that 53% of likely U.S. voters think it is fair to say that neither party in Congress is the party of the American people. George Washington issued a warning about political parties more than 200 years ago, saying they were destructive and could divide the country. Those sentiments reflect the views of the majority of the American people surveyed in a Gallup poll. According to the poll, 60% of Americans say the Democratic and Republican parties do such a poor job representing the American people that an alternative, third major party is needed.

Our two current parties would argue that our government simply was not set up for more than two parties and that there would never be a consensus if everyone voted on party lines. They argue that nothing would get done. May I ask, as citizen of this great nation...what the hell is getting done now? The parties choose their talking points and many, many big issues never even get put on the table let alone discussed.

More people every day our falling from both parties... drip by drip; drop by drop. The more parties stoke up their base the more voters they lose from the fringe. There aren't two umbrellas big enough to fit everyone's opinion on what needs addressed, especially if they have massive holes. Both sides talk of being inclusive but it seems more and more people don't want to be included in the Red or Blue. Younger voters especially cannot relate to either party. With 60% of Americans welcoming a third party. "These results show that the American people have finally had enough of a two-party system that so constantly works against their interests," writes Evan Lynne, a co-chair for "Young Greens," the youth caucus of the Green Party, and a student at the University of North Carolina-Greensboro. When I see such a high percentage, it gives me hope and further motivation to work with the Green Party."

The infighting in Congress disappoints Lesley Chan, president of Young Americans for Liberty (YAL) at the University of Nevada-Las Vegas. She founded her school's YAL chapter because she saw the need for a Libertarian group on campus. Chan thinks neither of the two major parties adequately reflects the views of the American people. She, too, says she would like a third major party to emerge, but she is unsure how three parties would function in the current political system. "I think what would be most practical would be for the Republican or Democratic Party — but most likely the Republican Party at this point — to adopt more socially liberal views so it would become essentially the Libertarian Party to go up against a left party," Chan says.

Younger conservatives could re-launch the Libertarian Party and the young progressives could do the same for the Green Party. The Tea Party has been a new kind of party that recently arose. There

Sign up for free voting resources at LouGarino.com

could always be a brand new third party take hold, or an Independent that aligns with a party to get on a national ticket. If a lightning rod of a candidate came out of a different arena, say a popular NFL coach or a man like Governor Jesse Ventura, it could immediately change the political landscape. First, they are known, they are proven leaders, they demand respect and have innate problem solving skills. But beyond that they are from the outside of power and voters could quickly see how their no nonsense approach could quickly translate into the skill set necessary to run our government. Their singular personality could launch a whole new momentum and, just like that, a new party could have new candidates on ballots all over America.

In our high tech world of viral possibilities, when a person could fall off a bike and get two million hits on YouTube, any amount of instant momentum is possible and a politician, out of nowhere, could go ballistic. How hard would it be to get people to leave their current party? Not very hard, aye? So for all the people that think we're destined for two parties for eternity, I've got news for them. Voter apathy could quickly become voter momentum when the situation is right. In America, voters are between disappointing and mad. When they become more mad than disappointed, voting apathy could disappear as we know it.

Fear and Loathing: Voting in America in 2016
an Anti-Partisan Apathy to Action Approach by Lou Garino

Chapter 5 – 2014

Fear and Loathing: Voting in America in 2016
an Anti-Partisan Apathy to Action Approach by Lou Garino

Voter Inspiration

The celebrities who would do "anything" to get people to vote

In a video released just before the election, actor Will Ferrell told fans that he would do "anything" to get them to vote for President Barack Obama.

Among other things, Ferrell offers to move your couch, give you a badly-drawn tattoo, and even dance for you!

Fear and Loathing: Voting in America in 2016
an Anti-Partisan Apathy to Action Approach by Lou Garino

Welcome to 2014

Our Phones – Wireless
Cooking – Fireless
Cars – Keyless
Food – Fatless
Tires – Tubeless
Dresses – Sleeveless
Youth – Jobless
Leaders – Shameless
Relationships - Meaningless
Attitudes – Careless
Babies – Fatherless
Feelings – Heartless
Education - Valueless
Children - Mannerless
Country - Godless
We are SPEECHLESS,
Congress is CLUELESS,
Our President is WORTHLESS
And, we're scared SHITLESS!

GOD HELP US!

Sign up for free voting resources at LouGarino.com

Fear and Loathing: Voting in America in 2016
an Anti-Partisan Apathy to Action Approach by Lou Garino

What the hell just happened in the 2014 Election? I'm not talking about the results, I'm talking about voter participation or lack thereof, and the effect big money had in the election's outcome. The bigger question is what can we learn from this and where is voting in America going to go from here?

Well, first thing is first. **People** just don't turn out for off year non presidential elections like they do for the big ones.... Period! When they do it's usually to vote against a candidate or a party. The polling stations have only the hardcore conservative never miss a vote people, and minorities and younger people just don't vote. That's just a hard fact. We heard it many times that we are a 60/40 country... 60 percent of eligible voters participate in presidential elections and 40 percent shows up in the off year elections.

Dark money has never been more of an issue in political campaigns and it just got worse. The United States Supreme Court held that the First Amendment prohibited the government from restricting independent political expenditures by a nonprofit corporation. The principles articulated by the Supreme Court in the case have also been

Sign up for free voting resources at LouGarino.com

extended to for-profit corporations, and other associations. There you have it... you think you saw sickening political ads before? The Koch Brothers have almost a billion dollars in their piggy bank ready to go in 2016. Talk about an unfair playing field. Who is electing the candidates in the primaries? Right at the time but where in the hell is it going to go? We'll have commercials twelve months a year.

Except for one little problem, those were the good old days. According to the United States ElecProject, the 2014 election had the lowest participation since World War II. Only 36.4% of eligible voters cast their ballot. With all that's on the line in our nation right now, and that's a whole lot, only slightly over a third of eligible voters bothered to pull the curtain and vote their conscience. It literally took a World War to keep more people from the polls then it did November 4, 2014. I guess the folks in 1942 had a few things on their mind, like their sons and daughters fighting, dying and serving in droves all over the World. If you weren't serving overseas in '42 you were battling on the home front. Men, like my dad, who were 4F, were working 60 hours a week to meet production. Women stepped out of the homes and into the factories and kicked ass. Rosie the Riveters, like my mom and all my aunts, went into the factories, matching the effort and skill to quickly become the epitome of efficiency. To this day, I know of no one as efficient as my Mother. So let's get this right, in 1942, with Americans working double overtime, with strong leadership and with a direct and common country mission, voted as much as we did in '14. Crazy, isn't it? What was there to vote for in '42? Even if you were not working a 16-hour shift, what was on the plate? There was a singular issue on the table...win the war or speak German! Yet these guys somehow still managed to vote as much as the citizens of America voted in 2014. That's right, virtually the same as our nation in 2014. Today our country is gripped in a never-ending war against terrorism, a war that will go on forever if we don't stop it. Our government is split on climate change, split on every single issue, it is split on itself. A house divided will surely fall. We are receiving no leadership, only noise, with reactive policies instead of vision; and there is no clear mission and certainly no direction.

In the 1964 election, nearly 59% of eligible electorate voted. It was the "Summer of Freedom" voter registration program and young voters were being registered at record paces. We talk on my radio

Sign up for free voting resources at LouGarino.com

show all the time about how passionate politics were in the '60s. Doesn't really matter which side you were on, you were engaged. The boomers were finding themselves and wanting to live in love and peace. Vietnam ended up dividing a nation; but the nation never took its eyes off Vietnam and the war ended. America never took our eyes off civil rights and we got the civil rights bill passed, the EPA, 18 year olds the right to vote, you name it. We kept our eye on major issues and somehow things got done. To not participate in voting and politics was not an option. Imagine if today we put our collective vision on immigration reform? What if we had our eyes on infrastructure or solar power? The way big oil has infiltrated, addicted and polluted the earth is suffocating. I believe if we found an issue big enough to unite us, the will of the people would be done. We as voters need paint a dream and must be willing to step toward it; to elect the people that bring the flow of power up from the people, to do what's right for all, not the select few.

In the 1960s and '70s there was dialogue at every kitchen table in America. I don't care what side you were on. Boomers were rapidly changing the political landscape with a growing progressive, not the "same as my parents" attitude with the morals to match. The old line stood the ground fighting change, and the boomers welcomed it as our country was hit on all sides with issue after issue.

A good example of this dialogue was captured by Norman Lear, the producer and creator of the early '70s show "All in the Family." Every episode the characters sat at the dinner table with Carroll O'Connor (Archie) and Rob Reiner (Mike), going at it hard, usually on the issues of the day. In many ways they represented their respective generational views, with Mike having progressive ideas with black and Latino friends asking hard social questions, and Archie hanging with his like-skinned buddies from the loading docks, going to the lodge and hanging onto their way of life. That fact they argued at the dinner table 'every night' is the key here. They were passionate about the issues, yell and scream but could respect each other enough to argue again the next day. There was a lot of passionate debate at the dinner tables back then. Television is more of a fabric of American lives now way more than it was 40 years ago when All in the Family aired.

Sign up for free voting resources at LouGarino.com

The reason I use All in the Family as an example is to show how much our television has changed and at the same time how much our voting has changed. I do not profess to know television today as I only watch it for the misinformation to study to actually find the facts. So are there any shows really hitting the issues that affect us like that show? I kindly doubt it! NO WAY would they even let that show on television today, no way. Do any shows on TV debate hard issues that are poignant and being voted on?? I didn't think so. So how is it there are 100x as many shows as there were 40 years ago, all saying less and less? If we're getting dummied down in our entertainment, what about our news? Yes, we are fed what they tell us. There is an old saying, if you were told lies 24/7, sooner or later you'll start to believe them.

Let's think about this for a moment, shall we? In 1964, information was very hard to get compared to today's standards. Network television was in its infancy and the three major networks limited their news programming to 30 minutes a day and local news affiliates. Even if they had news, it was also a 30-minute segment. Take out commercials, sports and weather, and you really weren't getting that

Sign up for free voting resources at LouGarino.com

much news. But the news you did get was close to actual news with a lot less fluff. Human interest stories? I remember seeing bloody wounded Vietnam soldiers being transported, screaming... every night! News was in your face. It hurt. In the '60s, Dan Rather was traveling with a platoon on missions battling live fire. Reporters today, while still in danger, are many miles from battle, usually making a report from a tall building with a cityscape in the background, hopefully with some flames to sell and wearing a black jacket for effect. If the media was allowed to cover the real war, showing our kids mutilated on the screen every night, our nation's imperialism would end quickly. The glut of looped information in the media is purposeful on the American psyche. We are easily lead to a confused state so that we are easily lead.

Back then, most affluent homes had access to current private libraries but most folks were just happy to have a set of encyclopedias, if they were that lucky. That certainly wasn't current information, was it now? There were of course school and public libraries but again, no current information there to speak of. However, Americans used to read these things called newspapers, magazines, and periodicals;

Sign up for free voting resources at LouGarino.com

and they read them cover to cover. The printed word had much more value toward forming objective opinion. News wasn't yet in the entertainment business and the people that brought it to you were not yet models but rather NEWS people. They really weren't selling anything back then except, well... news. In 2014, our news consisted of a 24-hour cycle of a mish mosh of people posing as experts, being aligned on panels, arguing a single issue at a time. Where did the news go? News shows just jump on something they are told to, throw it in the news cycle and beat it to death, all day every day until something else springs up. It's all ISIS and terrorism, all the time until...EBOLA!!! Or a no talent hack "celebrity" I won't dignify with a name... takes a pic of her ass, and boom another cycle of crap! Then...well... you know, rinse, repeat! Panel after panel, expert after expert...yada yada yada! NOISE NOISE NOISE! What can we sell the sheeple today? A whole lot of nothing. Like eating cheese puffs.... looks big and fluffy but with no substance, and disappears immediately for another and another. I've had many guests on my shows that have been on all the major news channels. Every one of them will tell you, if you want to go back on the shows, just tell them what they want to hear! Yeah, that's news.

Fear and Loathing: Voting in America in 2016
an Anti-Partisan Apathy to Action Approach by Lou Garino

There is disturbing growing evidence that the cable news and even the network news are part of government psychological operatives, forming opinion, propaganda and controlling public thought. Don't think it's possible? You better think again...TV is fixed. Look into this and see for yourself. They could be using props and making up everything and how would you know. Are you in Syria? Iraq? It could all be a big show to sell their war and scare America.

All this leads us to a place where we are in politics 2014. Americans are working harder for less than at any time in over a generation. Of course this allows less time to investigate real information on the issues. If you have less time to explore real news you are more liable to get it quickly in sound bites, and that is dangerous. You don't want to live in a sound bite world. People are reading less and less and it will continue to get worse; and that's good for the powers that be. The literacy rates in some areas are lower than they were during the Revolutionary War. While the internet provides the very best access to research for abstract thought and reasoning, most people use it for social networking or to investigate only the information that supports their preexisting views.

Sign up for free voting resources at LouGarino.com

Fear and Loathing: Voting in America in 2016
an Anti-Partisan Apathy to Action Approach by Lou Garino

What a shame to have the Library of Alexandria at your fingertips and you only want to read the funnies.

So what is going on in our country in 2014? With all the information everywhere, how and where are people getting their information that decides elections? I really think anger had more to do with the 2014 election than policy. I'll bet most people that actually voted studied very little on the opinions of the candidates. It seems that everybody everywhere is just pissed off that everyone they put into office is dropping the ball in the red zone. Partisan is out of control. Money is killing political equality and serving only special interest. Senators say "look at me" and stage nonsensical filibusters. We get not one but two government shutdowns... Yeah, that 113th Congress let the federal government of the United States shut completely down twice. The 114th Congress who have just been sworn in are threatening to shut down the government again. Where's the change we thought we were voting for? How does that strike the heart of the American voter who is already punchy from all the blows to head?

With every new group of officials we elect, it's almost like we have the hope of a major league

Sign up for free voting resources at LouGarino.com

baseball team in spring training. Sure we don't have all the pieces, but if some of these young guys improve, and the veterans can keep it together, get some mid-season help from the minors, we might magically pull the pennant out. Well, of course this team goes on to lose a hundred games that year. At least they wait until spring training is over before they show their incompetence. With the new 114th Congress threatening shut downs as soon as they were sworn in does not bode well for the prospects of them getting them getting anything done for the American People. The only time the legislature does get a bill passed is when they give away the store by attaching amendments and hurting Americans.

Do they really want people to drop out of the voting process? The way they're acting, it sure feels like it.

Chapter 6 - My Vote

Voter Inspiration

The displaced people who went out for mobile voting stations.

Dorothy Ann Van, of Long Beach Island, New Jersey, is currently homeless after her house was destroyed by Hurricane Sandy.

Her current situation did not stop her from finding a voting van and casting her vote...
In her bathrobe!

Fear and Loathing: Voting in America in 2016
an Anti-Partisan Apathy to Action Approach by Lou Garino

**DON'T VOTE?
DON'T COMPLAIN!**

Sign up for free voting resources at LouGarino.com

Fear and Loathing: Voting in America in 2016
an Anti-Partisan Apathy to Action Approach by Lou Garino

Looking back at life I find that politics Looking back at life, I find that politics was ingrained in me from the very beginning. My maternal grandfather was a coalminer who walked five miles to the mine every day before they could get a car in the '30s. He and his fellow miners fought hard for safety and worker rights, and he was a proud union man until the day he died. My fraternal grandfather was a small businessman and had a part in a small brewery as well. They were both first generation immigrants that saw America as the shining city on the hill, and that it was our privilege to be part of this great nation. I just can't remember my family ever not being involved in what was going on in politics at the time and voting their conscience. They weren't stepped on either side and that rubbed off on me. Whatever the election, there was no way you were keeping them from the polls. No way. Pride, honor and respect were the pillars of their lives and that of most of America.

I have been blessed with a memory that enables me to recall the '60s as if it were yesterday. Of course, I fact checked it but I had the whole nine yards because I lived it and I care. I remember the daily death count from Vietnam on the evening news with Howard K. Smith. Every night the screen was filled with horrific, unedited footage, soldiers screaming, bloody images, pain. I still think about this often. I remember the riots, demonstrations, Kent State, draft card burning and the TET offensive...the bombings and more bombs! I recall when soldiers, returning with honor from Vietnam, were cursed and spit on when they got off the plane. I remember when Martin Luther King Jr. was murdered. I'll never forget that night he was killed, when Bobby Kennedy spoke to an all-black audience and told them Martin had been killed by a white man. He said that he understood how they feel, because his brother was also killed by a white man. Against advice from his handlers, he didn't shy from speaking to them. His was a voice of reason, a man of privilege that found the plight of common man and even those who society forgot. I was a kid but I loved him!! He said a quote that night that I vaguely remembered and took me years to find. It's from a Greek playwright named Aeschylus "He who learns must suffer, and even in our sleep, pain we cannot forget falls drop by drop upon our heart, and through our own despair and against our will comes wisdom to us by the awful grace of God." That quote is his epitaph.

Fear and Loathing: Voting in America in 2016
an Anti-Partisan Apathy to Action Approach by Lou Garino

We brought the TV in the dining room for the first time ever the night he was shot. While I grew up hearing about JFK's assassination, it didn't have a relevance to my feelings. But I remember how I wept for this man, I'm not sure why but I had this feeling that he was the person to guide the country that I loved so much. After all, I could sing the star spangled banner when I was five, and have been singing it as loud as I can ever since. My young patriotic heart was broken and in a way, it feels reeling and yearning ever since.

I can't pretend to know the issues in the 1968 presidential election other than the Democratic incumbent Lyndon Johnson would not seek nor would he accept the nomination of his party to be the President. It seemed to be Republican Richard M. Nixon's time and he easily won over Hubert Humphrey. Looking back, it was the end for the New Deal Democrats, they had their run. 1968 was a major year in our nation's development. Our country's tumultuous problems were many and the vision for our great nation was as clear as mud. Somebody had to pay. George C. Wallace was holding on to hate and segregation and ran as a third party candidate. He was the last third party candidate to win a state. In the presidential election of 1968, he won Alabama, Georgia, Mississippi, Arkansas and Louisiana with the American Independent Party.

By 1972, things had settled down a bit and the economy had a pulse. Though he originally escalated the war in Vietnam, Richard Nixon now promised to end the conflict soon, and crushed his democratic challenger, George McGovern for president. In the largest blowout in American presidential history, Nixon carried every state but one and D.C. I remember the influence of the debates and how Nixon seemed in control. I was ten, we were going to the moon, unrest was down, and there seemed a flow to the country as Vietnam was winding down. Nixon had done just enough to keep a nation from imploding. It seemed our country finally had leader they could get behind and the President they had wished for. Be careful what you wish for your wishes may come true.

Soon after the '72 election however, things began to unravel like a 2000-year-old mummy. First our dear Vice President, Spiro Agnew, resigns amid charges of conspiracy, bribery, and extortion. Ah, Spiro the triple threat! Enter stage left, newly appointed Gerald Ford to the second highest position in the land, one scandal, ah, I mean heartbeat from being the leader of the free world. Son-of-a-gun, wouldn't you know it? It seems even before the '72 election, Richard "Tricky Dickie" Nixon had been playing dirty tricks on his opponent, like bugging his headquarters in the Watergate office complex in Washington D.C.

I remember coming home after school and watching the Watergate Hearings. I was getting older, around 11 or 12, and my "Bullshit Meter" was starting to develop while watching those guys squirm around questions. I really couldn't get enough of it. It was my country and I needed to know what was happening, and I want more people to feel that way today. As it developed we quickly found out that crap runs downhill, especially if it starts at the very top. On August 9, 1974, Richard Milhous Nixon, facing impeachment, became the first person ever to resign the Presidency of the United States.

Anyone alive in the early to mid-1970 remembers the beginning of the decline of manufacturing. Thanks to an OPEC oil embargo we had, remember waiting in a long ass line for gasoline in your 10 MPG car, and a brand new term for our economy: stagflation, where

Sign up for free voting resources at LouGarino.com

things are so bad you need to combine existing bad words. Well, good thing we had leaders of the people, by the people, for the people.

On August 9, 1974, Gerald Ford was sworn in as President of the United Sates, and John D. Rockefeller was sworn in as Vice President. Scary, a Rockefeller appointed to within a heartbeat from the presidency. Neither person received a vote from our citizens, not one vote. Ford took over an economy that was so bad they needed to create new words to describe it. Remember "Stagflation?" He immediately pardoned Nixon from all crimes, which emblazoned everyone but Nixon of course. Really? Let the crook off so easy? Then on April 30, 1975, the fall Saigon. The Vietnam War ended in disgrace. I can still close my eyes and see those people on the roof top waiting for the next chopper. ARGGGH.

For me, the presidential election of 1976 was the spark that lit the fire of liberty in my soul. I had grown up with nothing but war my whole life. My presidents had been shamed from office, promoted a war at a cost of 52,000 lives, and been assassinated. I remember feeling angst against the establishment, and how could I not? I still feel the pain of that war in my heart. I remember being enthralled with a smiling Washington outsider and peanut farmer from Georgia, Jimmy Carter. My ninth grade history class had a mock election with two delegates representing each party. I was the Democratic delegate for Carter in our class, and I professed change, I argued that we needed a new direction. We voted the same day as the presidential election, and the class chose Jimmy Carter. I think the results were 18-12, although I can't confirm. Some things you just can't google. The day of election, that night when the real votes were counted, the Country saw it the pretty much the same way. Jimmy Carter was the new president.

Now that my observation of politics was cued, I was paying much more attention to the goings on with our elected ones. But there wasn't much to pay attention to other than more stagflation, poor economy, and jobs being lost everywhere. Then in November 4, 1979, Iranian students took over the embassy and held 52 Americans hostage. Most people don't remember, but this was the start of a new program called Nightline to feed Americans' insatiable appetite for this story. Then the Soviets invade Afghanistan, we get mad, we boycott the Olympics, everybody gets mad... Well, Jimmy, at least you weren't crooked!

1980 was my very first election. I had been waiting a long time for this. On my birthday, July 28, I walked down the sunlit sidewalk of my home town and signed two documents: my voter registration and my selective service document. Although I couldn't vote in the primaries, I paid particular attention to them and the cast of characters involved. Really they were characters. Ed Kennedy was challenging Carter on the Democratic side, and the Republicans had the ultimate character of B movies with Ronnie, fresh off the set of a poor movie career followed by a great career as a corporate spokesman. A former Democrat, now Republican, a former union head now anti-union. George H. W. Bush, former head of the CIA, Bob Dole and a straight talking guy from Illinois, John B. Anderson.

My first political disappointment was Jimmie Carter, so to me he was out of the running for MY vote. Bobby Kennedy was one of my earliest political heroes, and I loved Edward Kennedy's ideas as an extension of his. The vision of one more Camelot was not to be, as Carter was the incumbent and Ed's closet was overflowing with things of a skeletal nature. Jimmy would be his party's candidate.

As I watched the Republican debates (yes I, as an 18-year-old, watched the debates) the only one that appeared to be actually answering the questions was John Anderson. The only one who actually admitted to making a political mistake was Anderson, as he said he regretted his vote on the Gulf of Tonkin Resolution, the false flag operation that enabled the U.S. to start the Vietnam Conflict. Just like 9/11 was a false flag operation to implement all the wars since and forever. While every other candidate was kowtowing to the NRA, Anderson stood before them and made a modest statement about licensing gun owners. He said that it was an important thing to do to get cheap guns out of the hands of criminals, mental incompetents, and convicted felons. All these years later he was spot on.

Ronald Reagan won the Republican primary and selected George H.W. Bush as his running mate. Jimmy Carter and Mondale were on the Democratic side. John B. Anderson ran as a third party candidate. I was not loving on Jimmy anymore and Reagan/Bush did not sit well with me, an actor and a spy. On the fourth day of November, 1980, I walked into the voting booth for the first time, pulled the curtain and voted for independent, John B. Anderson of Illinois. Ronald Reagan won in a landslide. I made my choice for the person I best thought for the job of president. I recently watched the 1980 presidential debate between Anderson and Reagan, Carter would not appear because of Anderson. THAT is exactly what is happening now with voices being ignored and the candidates looking the same, acting the same, only one wears home jerseys and the other away jerseys.

As if America was due grace, the hostages were released as Reagan was taking office; and of course it couldn't have started better for Dutch. He looked tough from the get-go. The country was looking for anything it could find to rally around and nothing better for that than beating up on the Commies...those damn Soviets.

The economy was due for an upswing and Reagan was in the right place at the right time. The country united again behind the flag as deals deregulating banks and corporations were done behind closed doors. The 1984 election had found the country in a somewhat different state of affairs. We were ten

Sign up for free voting resources at LouGarino.com

years removed from a war, and eight years before the next. We didn't know it at the time, but we were in the middle of the longest peace in 50 years and now maybe forever.

The 1984 election was basically just the country going through the motions. Reagan had everyone on his wagon and things were dropping in place. I was in college as a business student and I loved the deregulations and thought at the time that was the answer. Even though I knew he was a corporate puppet, I liked the guy. Had I known how his trickle-down economics didn't trickle to anyone, and how the separation of the classes started with him, I never would have been on his side. The best the Democrats could come up with in '84 was Walter Mondale. Even picking the first female running mate with Geraldine Ferraro he didn't have a chance in hell. It looked as if was going to be a landslide and it was. I liked Reagan and his brand of conservatism. In the 1984 presidential election I voted for Ronald Reagan/ George Bush.

The 1988 election was much of the same ole, same ole. Bush capitalized on a good economy and a stable international stage and easily won the

Republican nod. I remember the Democratic field being crowded that year with an uninspiring Michael Dukakis prevailing. Dukakis took an old statesmen senator from Texas, Lloyd Bentsen, as a V.P. running mate. Bush could have picked Mickey Mouse and won and he practically did with a pick out of nowhere with Dan Quayle? Who?

With an actual human as a Vice Presidential candidate, George H.W. Bush, the youngest fighter pilot in WW II, became president and he got my vote doing it. Bush easily won in a landslide in a race that Dukakis never seriously challenged. I recall liking the way Bush served as Vice President and I never really took Dukakis seriously. I remember Bentsen spanking Danny Boy in the V.P. debates but we don't vote for V.P.s. It was to be Bush's time, but not for long. His New World Order speech while he was in office really scared me as well as his signing of the United Nations Agenda 21. Giving the UN the right to declare Martial Law and bring in their peace keeping troops into our country. What is really scary is DHS has purchased in 2014, 1 million rounds of .223 caliber ammunition. The same caliber as the UN troops.

Fear and Loathing: Voting in America in 2016
an Anti-Partisan Apathy to Action Approach by Lou Garino

The calm elections in my life were over and I didn't even know it. 1992 brought in a whole new matrix to presidential politics. We were reading President Bush's lips about "No New Taxes" but he raised them anyway. Then we had this little squeaky guy from Texas, a billionaire outsider named H. Ross Perot. Then Slick Willie and his band of misfits came rolling out of Arkansas and connived his way through the field for the Democratic nominee.

The debates were great with a third party to shake it up. Perot was way ahead of the others as far as actually having a business like plan to lead America. No doubt for me William Jefferson Clinton couldn't keep his rocket in his pocket and had character issues, turned out I was right, I certainly wasn't voting for him. Bush had seemed to lose any mojo he ever had, especially with me. On Election Day 1992 I voted for the candidate that I knew would make America more stable, Ross Perot. He was actually leading in the polls that summer but inexplicably pulled out of the race for two weeks. He got a ton of votes but couldn't win a state and Clinton pounded out a victory.

Fear and Loathing: Voting in America in 2016
an Anti-Partisan Apathy to Action Approach by Lou Garino

1996 was to be the first time I would ever campaign in a presidential election, ninth grade withstanding. This election was to be the last call of the greatest generation when Bob Dole won the Republican nomination for president. Ross Perot was still around but not relevant as many of the issues he raised in '92, like the deficit, were being addressed and he was denied access to the debates.

In 1996, Bob Dole was a middle of the road Republican. A wounded war veteran and a long standing member of the Senate, Bob Dole was known as a man of conviction and reason. He was about as exciting as watching paint dry but a better man there was not. If it's one thing I loathe it's a slippery person. They'll say and do anything to get what they want. I don't see our fore bearers as slippery people and that is a standard I will keep through my voting life.

In the summer of 1996, I took my two-year-old son, Lorenzo, to a Bob Dole rally. He carried a sign that said "Babies for Bob" and that is how I got involved in a presidential campaign. I grew up with Watergate and I will first take integrity, thank-you please. I really liked Bob Dole. He really had a great message but America was in love with the young. Newer, faster, better they say. No one really listened to Bob and his message was lost. I voted for Bob but America once again voted for a man who was soon to be impeached because of a girl and a blue dress. I hate to say I told you so...The Clinton Club has been accused in a long torrid history of manipulation, drug dealing and even murder.

https://www.youtube.com/watch?v=vTIXRy7ssbI

Who will be the president in 2000?? It was told to me by a very credible source that right after the election of '96 the conservative elite gathered at a little known country club on the Laurel Mountains of Pennsylvania called Rolling Rock Country Club. It's an old, old money place started by the Mellon family that's way under the radar. They needed to implement their guy and make sure their world agenda would be met. To me, it's scary to think that this could be possible; but as I witnessed all the events unfold after I was told this in '97, I have little doubt that it was all true. So, who did they tell me would be the next president? Yes, George W. Bush. ...to which I said, "You're crazy!" He can't spell cat if you spot him the C and the T. Outside of Texas, who the hell will vote for him? They told me they had a close family member in the room and it was happening. I ask for their credentials and was overwhelmed at what I was given about their close family member. What I was being told would unfold like a nightmare for America, but perfect for what they needed to do: execute their agenda.

In the election of 2000, all gloves were off. Every prior election was a pillow fight compared to this one. The politics of dirt was escalated two fold from anything America had ever seen. With Karl Rove leading Camp Bush, they mercilessly beat down one candidate after another until they were the only one standing. I couldn't believe he won the Republican nomination, I couldn't believe what was happening, and it was only to get better.

Believe it when I tell you, I knew what would happen if Bush won this election. I knew he would be the puppet of puppets for the war machine and Wall Street, and the money that flows there. As bad as that appealed to me, it was with almost equal disdain that I held Al Gore. He was always so smug and cocky, still is. He was almost groomed for this and he felt entitled. He way underestimated the Bush machine and he never saw what was coming.

Sign up for free voting resources at LouGarino.com

Fear and Loathing: Voting in America in 2016
an Anti-Partisan Apathy to Action Approach by Lou Garino

The only one who talked to the people in the debates was Ralph Nader. Yes, Ralph Nader. He made too much sense on stage. Neither Bush nor Gore had any kind of response because they were owned by their parties and corporation, and he humbled them on stage. He had plans to reform Wall Street and corporate raiders; corporations that hide offshore money. Real reform, and real answers. Stop spending insane amounts on defense; we need help at home. Currently half the money we make goes to defense, and we're the only super power. Couldn't we do with 25% going to defense? Better yet, why isn't anyone talking about the missing 5 trillion, YES, 5 trillion, that's missing right now from the Pentagon in 2015. We're spending more on defense than the rest of the world combined and we're wasting (or it's being stolen) more than the rest of the world spends on their defense. Crazy Bad! This vote was going to be easy... In the 2000, I took my son to the poll and I pulled the lever for Ralph Nader.

Well, I'll never forget that night watching the results coming in, and Al Gore was declared the winner. My immediate thought was, "Whew!!!" As I sat there watching the news, I still wasn't settled for some reason. In no time at all it was announced on the air that they pulled Florida from Al Gore, and it was back in play. It was as if I was shot in the stomach! It's true! I didn't have to wait for the final results, I didn't have to wait on recounts or hanging chads or Supreme Court decisions. George W. Bush was going to be the president for the next eight years. The agenda and plan of the Neo-Conservatives, the 1%, would prevail; and what I feared the most would come to be. Just as the news that I received saying who would be the president, they never said who would win the election. The fix was in and if you don't know that, study it a little more. The people knew it. His motorcade was pelted with rocks at his inauguration.

To put this in fair perspective, I voted for and campaigned for a Republican just four years earlier. This book is not about political parties because I am not partial; I'm American and they're both failing us. It's about taking our power back, America, by the power of the vote. The 1% can only control if the 99% let them by not voting. In November of 2000, the deficit was paid, job growth was great, the economy was cooking, there was relative stability in the world. The house was in good order.

Page 101

Fear and Loathing: Voting in America in 2016
an Anti-Partisan Apathy to Action Approach by Lou Garino

On September 11, 2001 a false flag operation was perpetrated on the American people. This horrific event spawned a never-ending war against a worldwide enemy, guaranteeing that it will go on forever unless WE stop it. After, the government went straight to propaganda, perpetuating fear so that we can have our liberties taken that were provided by the constitution. 19 guys with box cutters did all this?? Bush put big brother on steroids and sent him to the gym. Homeland Security, FEMA, TSA, NSA... how did WE become the enemy of our own government? I'll take my chances with any terrorist any day than have this police state that's being developed. Why didn't Bush or Cheney want an investigation into 911? When they were forced to have an investigation, they wouldn't cooperate. When they were forced to appear and be questioned, they would only do so if they were together, and even then not under oath?

As time goes by, more and more evidence that cannot be ignored shows that explosives were used to bring down the World Trade Centers, including building 7, the overly fortified CIA Headquarters in New York that was never even hit by a plane. Architects and Engineers for 911 Truth has a full report that totally debunks the 911 Commission

Report. Anyone that questions the 911 Commission Report is called a nut, a conspiracy theorist or worse. Secrecy in a democracy is repugnant. So why are we afraid to do a real investigation? I don't know, but it seems strange that no one is looking into this as it deserves. Why isn't there a mass movement for the real truth? If it is like they say it is, then we'll have no problem with the results.

Following the events of 911, we have reports of weapons of mass destruction, lies, lies, and more lies. They draped their lies in fear and patriotism, wrapped a flag around it and set the war machine in motion with no bid contracts, including the Patriot Act, NSA, TSA, DHS and more propaganda. They didn't just tell us to be scared, they told us how scared to be with the color system... yellow, orange, red. Such B.S! Taking the eyes of America off the real issues, like nation debt climbing by the trillions to finance a wasted war of aggression, Wall Street raiders getting fatter than ever on deregulation, and gambling our money and our sacred liberties -which stood for over 230 years- being stripped down quickly in the name of safety. It was so Orwellian I couldn't stand it. Never did I think oppression could come so fast so soon. 19 guys with box cutters... half of which were later proven to be alive. Yeah, they did this, those terrorists, that's what they told us so it must be true. Keep showing the loop on TV with the planes hitting the towers, and repeat the word terrorist 5000 times, then throw Bin Laden in there a 1000 times for good measure. Smoke and mirrors, America; smoke and mirrors. Who is behind the curtain pulling the levers?

2004 was a pivotal election. I would watch the President of my country pray publicly for the dead soldiers of a useless, endless war that he and his war machine started. Ask the poor people of Iraq, who just happened to be born there, if we are liberators. Ask them, after we killed hundreds of thousands of innocent men, women and children, killed by collateral damage, and destroyed their entire country. The entire world went from feeling sorry for us to hating us for attacking a sovereign nation. It made me sick and it still does. The imperialistic "New American Century" signed by the warmongers in the administration was in full effect!

What can I do?? I can vote!! I can canvass! I can act!

Fear and Loathing: Voting in America in 2016
an Anti-Partisan Apathy to Action Approach by Lou Garino

Senator John Kerry from Massachusetts, a decorated Vietnam veteran, won over a crowded field to win the Democratic nomination to face Bush in the general election. Surely, our nation would see the errors of their ways and change the course of this runaway train. As in 2000, it was the dirtiest, smear election that Karl Rove and the Bush camp could muster. They went so far as to bring in actors to portray veterans that served with Kerry, telling everyone in the commercial that he was a coward, and that his Combat Medals were not earned. Really? From a guy, George W. Bush, that got grounded in the Air Force reserves because of a failed drug test for cocaine?

In the 2004 election, I voted for John Kerry and tried to talk everyone I knew into doing the same. As the results poured in, it looked like our country was just scared enough to re-elect Bush. It was the smallest margin of victory ever by an incumbent. However, it has been published by two separate newspapers that there is hard evidence that Ohio, therefore the election, was stolen, and that another election to keep George Bush and his New World Order machine rolling was fixed. Feel free to study any and all issues for yourself. Two elections for W.

and two fixed results. That will really get everyone juiced to participate in the next election. There are three things that can't be hidden: the sun, the moon, and the truth. I hope I live to see the day the truth comes out about all the lies we were told for eight years. America deserves it.

If the election was really stolen, why didn't Kerry scream bloody murder? One reason might be that both he and W. were both part of a secret society in Yale called the Skull and Bones. They are sworn to an oath above country, friends and even family. H.W. Bush and even his father, the Nazi Party financier, Prescott Bush, belonged to this most secret of clubs from which global industrialist have spawned. Kerry would get his turn later as Secretary of State to shape the world and secure his spot in world changing history, and the charting of the new world.

As of this writing, George Bush or Dick (Chicken Hawk) Cheney will not travel out of this country for fear of being prosecuted for war crimes, of which they are guilty. Cheney canceled a trip to Canada. I never thought I would see the day where our former President and Vice President can't leave the country. I hope they get what they truly deserve in this life or the next.

Fear and Loathing: Voting in America in 2016
an Anti-Partisan Apathy to Action Approach by Lou Garino

Four more years gave us escalated debt, global shame, thousands and thousands killed and maimed, more global shame and just to cap it off, right before he exited office, a little $700,000,000,000 parting gift to his friends on Wall Street. Nice that his deregulation allowed them to gamble and lose all our money! The day of the vote in the bailout bill, the American people called their representatives in record numbers to tell them to vote NO on the bailout, the next day it was turned down. It looked like the people spoke and was heard! A few days later, behind closed doors with no hearings, they slipped a 700-billion-dollar bill on the American taxpayer. Our voices silenced. When George Bush left office, the surplus he inherited turned into a 10 trillion-dollar deficit, unemployment was at a record high, two wars a half world away, making our country in fact less safe, and our constitution shredded in the name of freedom... I could go on of course but I'm already feeling queasy. The house he walked into that was in pristine condition was now in shambles. We may never recover as a nation from the harm this administration did to the soul of our nation and militarization of the world.

Fear and Loathing: Voting in America in 2016
an Anti-Partisan Apathy to Action Approach by Lou Garino

The election of 2008 was an election of two paths. American was sick and tired of being sick and tired. The Republicans had John McCain, Mitt Romney, and Ron Paul at the top, and the Democrats had a crowded field, but really it was between Obama and Hillary Clinton. I loved watching the Republican debates because you had everyone saying the same thing except a Congressman from Texas, Dr. Ron Paul. Paul was speaking to my heart about our broken foreign policy, our country being taken over by corporations, and the ever shrinking of the middle class. He was ignored by the press, and even though he won states by votes, the delegates also ignored him and cast for mostly McCain. Paul was the brightest and best but he didn't have a chance against the Republican election machine who couldn't keep him in tow. The press/media is owned by six corporations. Do you think they want the candidates with the best ideas or the candidates that have the most money to spend on commercials? I thought you'd say that. There goes Ron Paul! The worst thing they could do, they did; they ignored him.

The Democratic field whittled down to Hillary and Barack, with each having a message of change. As the cycle wore, it was neck and neck until Clinton pulled out late. Her entitled attitude just wears on the regular people who are so graced to have her among us. Obama sold the hope and change message with the style and grace of a southern preacher. His speaking mannerism are those of the trained actor he is. It was enough to edge out Clinton II. Yes, an African American would lead the Democrats and be a major party nominee for the first time in U.S. history.

So there it was: Obama vs McCain. I liked McCain in 2000 until the Bush machine chewed him up like bubble gum. Like many in our country, after eight years of misery, were needing a dose of peace, hope and change. I had Obama slightly ahead of McCain but I was waiting to see who they would select as their V.P. and to see how things would shake out. My concern was McCain keeping the wars going. Turns out they kept them going and then some.

As the election progressed it was clear that Obama was 'speaking' to the middle class about frozen wages, raising healthcare costs, Wall Street bailout and the fact he didn't vote for the war in the first place. When John McCain picked Sarah "The thrilla from Wasilla" Palin it was all over. Sorry guys, she can't even form and speak coherent sentences.

Fear and Loathing: Voting in America in 2016
an Anti-Partisan Apathy to Action Approach by Lou Garino

On Election Day in 2008, I pulled the lever for Barack Obama/Joe Biden with hope of a new direction, but would we get it? I kindly doubt it. We ordered a Rueben sandwich and got a grilled cheese!

The weakest economy since the great depression chugged along leaving all the money at the top and only at the top. The wars began to fade with exit strategy in place. That exit would become more like a reshuffling of soldiers, and resources along the military trail protecting the oil and gas in the Middle East. The exit may never really come to pass. Real estate across the nation crashed as home values continued to fall, and foreclosures skyrocketed as predatory lending practices, allowed to flourish in the last administration, came to fruition. We had to go down a little farther before we could come back. The house was badly broken and needed leadership to repair it. My face is turning blue as I hold my breath awaiting the leadership's arrival.

The election of 2012 found the country as divided as it had been in a long time. Hard red, hard blue. There were no third party candidates to bring new ideas; just the same old partisan line. Gridlock was the way of Washington, and the winners are the corporations playing the loopholes and betting on both sides. The change and hope of '08 now just seemed muffled down to the same old "take what you get and like it." The economy was showing signs of life, but only for the few. The wars were winding down, but not really. There were messes everywhere, with a congress set on doing nothing and a president that went on a power grab like none in history.

The best the Republicans could come up with was Willard "Mitt" Romney, billionaire elitist that made a career out of running for president. This after buying, dismantling and selling off companies, sending tens of thousands of jobs overseas so he could make a fortune on the backs of American's pension funds. Wow, sign me up for this guy; I'm sure he'll be fair. Mitt looked like the poster child for a 1950s all-white male boardroom. His V.P., Paul Ryan, looked like a hungry pit bull that couldn't wait to gut social security and give even more tax breaks to the rich.

Given the choice (well, if you could call it that), there was no way I was giving my country to these Wall Street loving corporate raiders. Obama was not the leader anyone thought he'd be or hoped if I may. He was leading from the back seat, but managed to get the jobs bill through that started our country rolling again. However, with every recovery since Reagan, the middle class has shrunk; it's just a fact. Since his arrival, the Republican Congress treated him with the constant beat down and with such seething disdain you could almost call it hatred. In 2014, I voted for Obama/Biden.

I'm so disappointed in Obama ever since. Without another election, he is going rogue with executive order after executive order. Just to get the 2015 budget bill passed, just to pay our bills, Congress dropped all the regulations on Wall Street that were imposed after the 700-billion-dollar bail just seven short years ago. How can this be? Obama turns on his party and labor and fast tracks the worst trade agreement in history, the Trans Pacific Partnership. You knew something stunk when the Republicans praised him. Affordable healthcare is anything but. It is separating money and care, and giving the money to the insurance companies. Yes, more people pay for insurance but less people actually are covered. Insane! And our dear President just loves his predator drones.

Sign up for free voting resources at LouGarino.com

Fear and Loathing: Voting in America in 2016
an Anti-Partisan Apathy to Action Approach by Lou Garino

You saw my voting in the nine presidential elections. My record: four wins - five losses. Three Republican votes; three Democrat votes; and three Independent votes. It doesn't get more even than that, folks. So when I tell you I'm an American first and I'm mad as hell at them all, you can see that I'm talking the talk and walking the walk!

Let's hope whoever wins the presidency in 2016 will guide our nation to our founding principles, and not the way we're heading. Every day we get further from what makes our nation great, our Constitution. We can't lose our liberties in the name of safety. We cannot continue this insane distribution of wealth. We can't continue our imperialistic ways around the world, spending more on defense than all other nations combined. WE can't have 14 million children living in poverty in the greatest nation on Earth, and 50 million without health care, as we spend twice as much per capita as anyone else on it. We have real problems, and we need a real President for all of America.

In 2016, look first at where the candidate's money is coming from. Look at their total track history. Look at where they have come from, and who they have partnered with. Look for everything you can; ask the hard questions and demand the specific answers. Above all, hold whomever is elected accountable for their every action.

Chapter 7 - Conclusion

Voter Inspiration

The voters who endured over 2 hours and freezing lines.

In many cities, like Boston metro area, people waited in line for over 2 hours in freezing temperatures to cast their votes.

I

DON'T

CARE.

Sign up for free voting resources at LouGarino.com

Fear and Loathing: Voting in America in 2016
an Anti-Partisan Apathy to Action Approach by Lou Garino

Writing and fact checking my memory for this book brought out all my passion I have for this country I love so much. It hurts me to see the people we elect run our country, and run it to the ground. These people did not appoint themselves, someone had to vote for them. If we keep voting for the same ole, same ole, it's giving our permission to keep mucking it up. If we are to turn the tide on the systemic failure government and the people that comprise it, we must pass the barely lit torch to the children of today and our future. We must give them the tools and passion they need to brighten the flame of freedom; and to carry it to following generations until we have an engaged and educated electorate. I'm banking on kids to pull us out of this mess and I'm aiming to change the dynamics of our society by teaching two things to our kids: civic and fiscal responsibility.

Let's equip our kids with the skills necessary to be good citizens, not subjects; capable of open thought, discussion, and even decency if the need arises. We need to civically prepare our youth that a democracy is only as good as the people who live in it; that we need to remind all the federal agencies that they work for us, and somehow, some way we could vote them into extinction! We must show our youth that personal responsibility and accountability are paramount in the lives of Americans; that voting is a sacred right given to us by those that gave everything to secure it. Voting cannot be ignored, it is to be cherished and executed.

We need to make sure our school systems teach the skills necessary for a stronger democracy. If your state is enrolled in the Common Core program, I suggest you do whatever you can to get it repealed. It is mind melting our kids. When did it become the federal government's job to tell us how to educate our kids in our own states? I call to all our concerned citizens to get involved by volunteering to teach the power of voting to classrooms, clubs and libraries. With so much at stake, we need to get kids passionate, asking questions and needing answers. As generations grow, they will inherently want to be fully engaged in the politics of their time. Once on track, it's just a matter of time until we have a concerned, functioning government for all of our nation's people and generation after generation of conscious, engaged Americans.

Fear and Loathing: Voting in America in 2016
an Anti-Partisan Apathy to Action Approach by Lou Garino

It is not just our right to question authority, it is our obligation!

Sign up for free voting resources at LouGarino.com

Chapter 8 – Orwellian State

Fear and Loathing: Voting in America in 2016
an Anti-Partisan Apathy to Action Approach by Lou Garino

Voter Inspiration

The astronauts who vote from space.

Using a digital ballot on the International Space Station, NASA allows Americans to cast their votes for the presidential election while orbiting 240 miles above the earth. The ballot is securely sent to Mission Control, where it is transmitted to the voting authorities.

Space voting was authorized in 1997, but few have done it.

BAD
POLITICIANS
★★★
ARE ELECTED BY
GOOD PEOPLE
**WHO DON'T
VOTE**

Sign up for free voting resources at LouGarino.com

Fear and Loathing: Voting in America in 2016
an Anti-Partisan Apathy to Action Approach by Lou Garino

We live in a police state, with absolutely no doubt, especially for men of color. Take a hard look around you. Law enforcement and communities they represent have never been more disconnected, especially in urban areas. Military vehicles and combat vehicles rolling down American streets, by Americans to be used against Americans... Really?? Wire taps and surveillance everywhere, on almost every red light is a camera. Our government raped our constitutional rights "temporarily" in the slammed through Patriot Act, after our new Pearl Harbor of 911. That act enabled our "leaders" (specifically the Executive Branch) to launch the never-ending "War on Terror." If you think that 19 guys with box cutters did all this, you're wrong. Our elected officials did all of this, on our watch. And we let them. This story is so unreal it should be in the fiction section, but it's not. It's so Orwellian, I'm getting sick.

The "Home of the Free" is by far the most incarcerated nation on Earth, and now we're building and filling up FOR PROFIT prisons... Yeah, great idea there! Let's make money warehousing our citizens. This after already housing over 1,000,000 non-violent offenders, mostly because of archaic drug laws, or even unpaid fines??? Really? Yes, every day, people

Sign up for free voting resources at LouGarino.com

have warrants issued because they don't have enough money to pay a fine, say for driving without having auto insurance. People don't even have money for the insurance and now they have a huge fine they can't pay. They get their insurance back but can't get the money for the fine, and the warrant goes out for their arrest. That puts them on the run from the law. If they get pulled over going to work or just get shook down for looking suspicious while walking down the street, they're going to jail. Record! Lose job! Bail! Repeat! One in three Black men will be locked up.

I'm 52 and I remember where I was when Martin and Bobby were wasted like it was yesterday. Sitting in our dining room, pouring over the images on our 19" black and white Zenith on each instance. I grew up in a bitterly divided nation, so all this divisiveness is not new to me. What we are coming to now, however, is a different fear than we faced in the 60s. We no longer fear communism talking over the world or nuclear proliferation as much. Our biggest concerns now are right in our back yard, by the very people sworn to protect and serve us: the NSA, CIA, TSA, Homeland Security, with a healthy scoop of

Militarized Police and Industrialized Racism to top it off.

We see police brutality now on a mass scale by a few bad systemic cops and that hurts. But what really hurts is, in 2014, in America, it enrages many but it surprises no one. It's a microcosm of our current American experience.

People, especially minorities, wanted to see justice come to yet another young, unarmed, Black man dying at the hands of the police. Prosecutors refuse adamantly to ever really investigate, let alone prosecute. The FBI doesn't even keep track of how many citizens die at the hands of law enforcement each year. Again and again, justice is denied like a bad check returned for insufficient funds. Our justice systems is not set in stone; we can change it. We can make it better with each generation, but it isn't easy. We are dealing with an entrenched injustice system.

Department of Homeland Security, Transportation Safety Administration, FEMA, are all designed with controlling Americans in mind. Why has FEMA built camps all over the U.S. with barbed wire around them? Why did the DHS order one billion rounds of ammunition? Why are we still being illegally wire tapped? Has the TSA made us any safer or will they just continue to grope us for no reason? We know they failed their safety test, so why are they there? Why do these departments even exist? When I was a kid, our teachers said that in communist USSR, there was a soldier on every corner, and that encouraged citizens to tell on each other, and even for children to rat on their parents. Well, guess what we have right now? Could it be? Yes, every single one of these agencies is designed to keep us in line and not get out; no dissent, and no questions, just do what you're told!

As a nation, we have veered off the right path more than once on many issues, but somehow we have always become involved enough to turn it around. This is how we got out of Vietnam, and it's how we can start to square up this insane injustice in the name of justice. Let's not be the first generation to drop the ball. We clearing are at a major turning point. Our nation is only as good as the people who foster and care for it, and by the way that's US... Quit watching mindless entertainment shows posing as news shows and start reading, thinking and VOTING! Change need participation. Concerned citizens of our great nation, especially disenfranchised young people

(18-35), need to stand up and engage this political process, lest we live with the ever growing alternative.

VOTE=CHANGE

Sign up for free voting resources at LouGarino.com

Chapter 9 - Final thoughts

**NO MATTER HOW PARANOID
OR CONSPIRACY MINDED
YOU ARE,**

**WHAT THE GOVERNMENT IS
DOING IS WORSE THAN
YOU IMAGINE.**   W.BLUM

Fear and Loathing: Voting in America in 2016
an Anti-Partisan Apathy to Action Approach by Lou Garino

Right now our nation faces major challenges on so many levels. The world around us is much more unstable now that we went and smacked the Middle East bee hive with a stick. Our tax structure is great, if you're rich or a corporation doing business off shore. The two parties have calloused a nation and, with the help of the media, split our nation into a splinter of half red, half blue. There lies a palpable cauldron of division where reasonable debate seems to no longer exist. It certainly doesn't exist between the parties anymore, but the disheartening thing of it all is that it doesn't even exist between neighbors anymore. Opinions for some reason have turned unpatriotic when, at this point in our nation's history, that is exactly what is called for. It is the ultimate patriotism. It is what our country was founded on. As each election cycle passes, we get further from the very Constitution that has done us so good for so long.

America has a horrific infrastructure that will soon be exposed, as bridges start collapsing, gas and water lines blowout, and rolling blackouts become a norm. Our immigration policy is a disgrace, period! Students are burdened with crippling debt just to get a degree, and enter a work force where it probably won't be put

Sign up for free voting resources at LouGarino.com

to use. We have corporate tax loopholes that allow American companies to set up an address overseas and avoid taxes. I wish we could do that. We have chemical companies taking over the biological reconfiguring of well, everything, we know; and a FDA that fast tracks whatever they want regardless if it hurts Americans or not. We have a revolving door between Goldman Sachs and the Secretary of Treasury where former or even current CEOs are routinely made Treasury Secretary. Our lawmakers are in office forever, and if they do leave, they become a lobbyist, getting money from their former buddies and feeding the biggest corporation in the world. We have Big Brother all up in our grille, cooking our chicken. Even George Orwell would be shocked.

Okay, I can go on and on, but we need to address solutions to this crisis, and yes, it's a crisis! We as a nation are at a crossroads of epic proportion. If we continue to allow our politicians to run this course, our republic won't last but a few more generations, and we could quickly become a police state. Don't think it's possible? Just follow the breadcrumbs to where we are now compared to 20 years ago. Unconstitutional check points by federal agents under

Page 132

the excuse of immigration. TSA probing your ass just to get on a plane, making everyone just a little more scared. Homeland Security. This one really scares me... we no longer have a right to a trial if they think you're a terrorist. They can detain you permanently. Yes, this includes Americans. Thank you, Mr. Obama, for continuing what those before you have started; and chiseling away at our liberties. What makes terrorists different from someone who kills ten people in a rampage? Chipping away at the stone, they are.

The ONE thing we can do, the very one thing to save our nation, is VOTE!! The 1% is an exclusive club whose share of the pie is rising rapidly as the rest of ours shrinks. But the 1%, even with the billions to throw at an election, only have 1% of the vote, WE, you and I, own 99%!! People, it's as easy as thinking and learning and participating. Within a few election cycles, this could all be turned around.

We must demand our representatives do our will or they would be one and done. Hold them to their word. We need to get better candidates that are from the people, not plants from the corporations or parties. Let's start thinking at this differently since what we have is not working at all. Less attorneys

Sign up for free voting resources at LouGarino.com

and more business people, dentists, managers, even former NFL coaches. Government works easy if you line up teams to work together. America needs candidates that want to serve their region after a successful career, not making a successful career out of Washington for decades.

We must pick candidates from within our district and within our world, people that we know of, people we can get behind. The only way to get people in towns like Ferguson to vote is give them a candidate they feel is worth voting for. Give them someone they feel represents them. As soon as that happens, they get to see that government is from them, not over them. Cultures could change quickly and the separation they feel from government could start fading.

Term limits must be implemented. Seems that all candidates want term limits until they are elected. These people have been in office so long they are entrenched in their bitter opposition for each other. They are like sixth graders that will never ever, no matter what, cross my heart hope to die, never like each other. GET THEM OUT because they won't go on their own. Most of these guys have been there for

Page134

decades and some look like they died but didn't fall over yet. Anyway, they ain't cutting the mustard. Term Limits alone would change the dynamics of the people attracted to running for office. Gridlock assures reelection because you can always blame the other guy and it's darn hard to beat an incumbent. If you know you're only serving two terms, you would probably want to get more done. They certainly wouldn't be on a permanent campaign mode. If we get term limits, all the rest of the things that need to happen could go quickly.

We must ban forever electronic voting machines, a 4th grader could tell you that!

We must end former Congressmen going to work as lobbyists for Wall Street, Big Pharma, Dow chemicals and the whole heap that spend billions lining the pockets of the legislatures coffers. We must insist of our candidates that they must change the law to end this tragic bending of Democracy. It wouldn't hurt to make them pledge to never be a lobbyist. WE are not subjects, we are citizens and they work for us, and we need to be conscious enough to let them know that.

Page 135

Fear and Loathing: Voting in America in 2016
an Anti-Partisan Apathy to Action Approach by Lou Garino

Right now our voting system is being manipulated by delegates and the Electoral College system. Both must end for voter equality. Just because your candidate got the most votes in your precinct, it doesn't mean that delegate has to vote for your guy. That's what happened to Ron Paul over and over, and countless candidates over the years. For every vote to matter, and I thought that's what it is all about, this current system must end. Think about it: in Texas and California for instance, presidential candidates don't even stump there. Those states are decided before the election begins, so why should a candidate even address the issues that affect those states? It's unfair for all the states that aren't borderline. Eliminating the Electoral College and delegates puts the whole country on even ground and makes sure every vote counts. How do you change this? Get signatures, and get it on the ballot. Demand your candidate see it the same way. I really could do a whole book on this subject alone, but let's say its time has come to end.

Turn off your TV!! Put the remote down and QUIT getting your noise from that screen. They are melting your brain with soundbites and censored, edited discussions that somehow serve as news. There are a whole bunch of smart people that write articles every day, go find them and read them PLEASE! All information on the screen is owned by six companies. Yes, only six! Where there was once 100s of media outlets, the FCC let them form an oligopoly right in front of our eyes. There is nothing on the television that has anything to with news, not the real news. It's all filtered to get their message out, certainly not the news. For heaven's sake, watch the programs your kids are watching. They aren't as innocent as you think, especially shows on Disney where parents are often used as a punchline to jokes, and the cute little Disney girls like Miley Cyrus, Christine Aguilera et al. turn from sweet tweens to total sluts and take your daughters with them for the ride. Wake up, smell the truth, and shut it down! Now.

Our two party system is broken... Everyone knows it, but nobody ever does anything about it. Our two parties tell us a third party would slow down the wheels of democracy. Well then, how fast are they moving now? We need fresh ideas, fresh solutions and we need them now. We are not getting anything from our boys in red and blue. We must demand that networks allow equal footing to third party candidates at the debates. Why do the networks decide who will

Sign up for free voting resources at LouGarino.com

debate for our nation's highest office? Oh, that's right, they only give you what they want. Not if everyone called them and demanded another candidate be put on that stage. Most people today under 40 do not feel either party represents them. More and more voters are transitioning away from party affiliation. If we could get more third party candidates, the range of issues that would have to be dealt with in the public eye would finally start getting the discussion that it needs. I'm ending this chapter about taking back America with a quote from the Father of our great nation, George Washington, on his fear of a two party system taking over our government:

"The alternate domination of one faction over another, sharpened by the spirit of revenge, natural to party dissension, which in different ages and countries has perpetrated the most horrid enormities, is itself a frightful despotism. But this leads at length to a more formal and permanent despotism. The disorders and miseries, which result, gradually incline the minds of men to seek security and repose in the absolute power of an individual; and sooner or later the chief of some prevailing faction, more able or more fortunate than his competitors, turns this disposition to the purposes of his own elevation, on the ruins of Public Liberty. Without looking forward to an extremity of this kind, (which nevertheless ought not to be entirely out of sight,) the common and continual mischiefs of the spirit of party are sufficient to make it the interest and duty of a wise people to discourage and restrain it."

Fear and Loathing: Voting in America in 2016
an Anti-Partisan Apathy to Action Approach by Lou Garino

Chapter 10 – 2016 Addendum

IF OUR VOTE DIDN'T MATTER NO ONE WOULD WORK SO HARD TO KEEP US FROM VOTING

Fear and Loathing: Voting in America in 2016
an Anti-Partisan Apathy to Action Approach by Lou Garino

Mercy. Here we are at a moment in time in the United States history where big money is ruling everything. Wall Street, Big Pharma, Big Chem, Big Banks, Big Health Insurance, and Big Donors are running our nation into the ground for everyone but themselves. We are about to be flooded with the most expensive election in history; the "Hill" estimates the candidates will spend five billion dollars on the 2016 election. How we determine who represents our own best interest, our communities and our nation? I believe all major candidates have entered the ring so, since this is my book, I'm going to tell you what I think of each one. I didn't just start looking at these characters yesterday, I've been following them since they were on the scene.

Like many Americans, my opinion of what's best for our country has changed over the years. For example, when I was in college studying business in Southwestern Pennsylvania, I knew a lot of steel workers who lost their jobs. I felt that maybe their lucrative contracts contributed to the demise of the American Steel Industry; so while I still supported unions, I also saw that they may have contributed to the problem. I was wrong! Our own government allowed steel to be imported from foreign countries that subsidized their steel industry, thence, "dumping" their steel at an unfair price and putting our very own industry out of business, certainly NOT the fair wage the USW negotiated for their workers. Things are never what they appear, and sometimes it takes a while to figure it out.

40 years ago, approximately 40% of American Jobs were union; today it is 7%. Some states have tried banning organized labor. Why? Americans have never been working harder for less, even though our production has never been higher. Do you think the decline of the unions and the rocket rise in the income gap is a coincidence? I believe in wealth and the ability to obtain it, if you can make it, make it! I don't believe in a crooked playing field where the deck is immediately stacked against you. The days of thinking that anyone can make it to the top regardless of their social stature, if they just work hard enough, is no longer true in the greatest nation. Our school systems, mass incarceration, trillion-dollar student debt and a weak job market make it all but impossible except for the very few.

I am going to run down the list of candidates with a brief synopsis of each one and my frank, personal thoughts on each one. You don't have to agree, in fact, I hope you don't, because critical debate is what we need most. Don't just take my word, look for yourself and vote! The nation will thank you, and you will have earned your citizenship.

Candidates are in alphabetical order: Major Contributors; Comments.

Democrats:

Lincoln Chaffee- former New Hampshire Governor- raised $34,000 in last quarter. Sir Hillary raised 45 million last quarter! 'Nuff said. Another lame ass just trying to get a book deal out of it. Politico called her.

Hillary Clinton- Former First Lady, former New York U.S. Senator, former U.S. Secretary of State- Citi Group, Goldman Sachs, JP Morgan, Morgan Stanley, Time Warner, Cablevision and Lehman Brothers. Where do we begin with Hillary? Let's start with the aforementioned list of major contributors. Does it look like Wall Street or financial reform would come on Hillary's watch?! Politico called her, "Wall Street Republicans Dark Secret- Hillary in 2016." With her other top contributors, do you see your internet and cable bills continuing to skyrocket, with more and more mergers and less and less competition? She's been around so long that the people that do like her have no idea why or what her crazy voting record is. Watch the trail of corruption and entitlement that surrounds the "TEAM C." She actually took $200,000 from the Boys and Girls for a speech in Long Beach, CA and snuck off without speaking to the kids that it was supposed to benefit. The event was a $94,000 loss for the club. Does anyone, and I really want to know, believe she has a strong stance on any issue facing the real people of this country? She has been flip flopping like a guppy since she first arrived on the political seen, using polling to dictate her stance de jour. I swear she does a poll just to see what pant suit she'll wear. She talks the talk, but doesn't come close to walking the walk. All the news outlets however, will LOVE her and let her slide on just about everything. They will probably even jam up her competition because of her very bloated coffers for the endless commercials about to unfold in the general election. Clinton's election, should she win the nomination, will spend almost two billion dollars. How much money would they lose if say, Bernie Sanders, won the Democratic nomination? Think about that as the election unfolds, remembering that six oligopolies own 90% of what you see and read.

Martin O'Malley- former Maryland Governor. It appears he's tapping into his friend's pocket for poster board money. With no big money people getting behind him, he has little chance of lasting long. Like many governors, O'Malley has very little name recognition outside his state and region. He will likely fold early and never get out of single digits with voter appeal.

Bernie Sanders- Former Mayor Burlington VT, former Congressman Vermont, Current (I) Vermont Senator. Machinists/Aerospace Union, Teamsters, National Education Association, United Auto Workers, Communications Workers of America. Bernie is a Democratic Socialist. He doesn't hide from it; in fact, he proudly professes it. He is the longest serving Independent in U.S. congressional history. As an Independent he is seeking the Democratic nomination for President. At first glance, the thought of any type of socialism in our country would be horrific. Like most things we're not familiar with, we fear them. His model is based on countries like Sweden, Norway, and Denmark. Those countries have healthcare as a right, and I don't see a problem with that. We already spend twice as much per capita as any other nation and our healthcare sucks, really! It's good for some, but if we're already spending the money, let's actually spend it on paying doctors, nurses and staff, not healthcare CEO's 100s of millions. His message of this country belonging to all of us, not just a handful of billionaires, is resonating with voters. Many, many of the issues that Sanders argues in favor for has an approval rating with 70% of America. Sanders message has been consistent for 30 years, from voting no on the Iraq war, to no on the Trans Pacific Trade. The crowds for his speeches are overflowing with enthusiastic people wanting real change in our country. As I said earlier in this book, change will not come from just an election, change must come from a revolution of people, from such a large grass roots movement that it can't be ignored anymore. Could this be the candidate that ignites change? Washington insiders don't want him, the networks don't want him, Wall Street, big pharma, and the Koch brothers, surely don't want him. By the looks of all who hate him, I'm starting to like him on that alone and maybe a lot more. We'll see at election time.

Sign up for free voting resources at LouGarino.com

Fear and Loathing: Voting in America in 2016
an Anti-Partisan Apathy to Action Approach by Lou Garino

Jim Webb-former senator Virginia, former Secretary of Navy- contributors; University of Virginia, Goldman Sachs, Time Warner, Dominion Energy- Webb has little recognition outside Virginia, with little appeal. His early message about bringing the party to the right doesn't seem to be registering. With the looks of his donors, he could hang in there for a while but will never break from behind.

Now here's the Republicans: Most all of them.

John Ellis "Jeb" Bush- former Florida Governor- Jeb is trying to be the third U.S. President from the House of Bush and complete the Bush trifecta for the new world order. The vast dark caverns from which his campaign money could literally be printed is endless. Let's see, his brother, W., gave a 700-billion-dollar bailout to Wall Street in '08. So put down all the "too big to fail banks" for some dough. Defense contractors are lined up with full wallets as well as Big Pharma, Big Chemical, Big Communication and Big Corporations. Jeb and the Bushes are not in the Saudi's pocket; they are in their bed. Jeb's Daddy still gets daily briefings from the CIA, his old team, and also has a direct line with the Saudi Royal Family. I'm sure nothing secret ever comes up. As hard as this is to believe, Jeb has his brother, George W. "Mission Accomplished" Bush, on his Middle East advisory staff. In 1997, in response to the fall of communism and Clinton's foreign policy, a neo-conservative group designed a global plan calling for America to establish a "New International Order." It was called "Project for the New American Century." It called for the removal of Suddam Hussein and the installation of U.S. bases across the Middle East, protecting oil and gas reserves. They concluded that their plan had little chance of fruition, barring another Pearl Harbor. Among the 25 people who signed it, ten worked in the Bush Administration including: Dick Cheney, Cheney's chief of staff, I. Scooter Libby (prison), Donald Rumsfeld, Paul Wolfowitz AND John Ellis "Jeb" Bush. A little over a year after Jeb gave his brother, W., the presidency in the Florida recount, while we were sleeping, they got the Pearl Harbor they needed on September 11, 2001! Another Bush in power? God help us.

Dr. Ben Carson- Director of Pediatric Neuro Surgery Johns Hopkins: Dr. Carson has his own PAC National Draft Ben Carson Committee that has raised over 10 million coming into this year. He has written six bestselling books and is killing it on the speech circuit, playing to the band and picking up steam. He has never held a political office, which I believe is a huge plus. This is exactly what this book is calling for. Someone brilliant and impeccable from outside the political scene, someone who can use common sense and courage, who will take real stands on lifelong convictions, not polling. He has stated that we need to get big insurance out of medicine, I think he would know. He was raised by a single mom in Detroit, and was chief surgeon at 33. These are the type of candidates that can raise the bar and shape policy. We don't know much about him other than his "Truth to Power" speech at the National Prayer Breakfast with President Obama looking on from five feet away in disdain. You want to know Ben Carson, take time to YouTube his speech:

https://www.youtube.com/watch?v=PFb6NU1giRA

I can't wait to hear him in the debates. I'm rooting for this guy and I can't wait to see how his campaign unfolds as America gets to know him

Chris Christie- Current Governor New Jersey- Christie is THE corporate spokes piece, so raising money will not be a problem. His New Jersey Governorship reads like a Soprano's episode with

Sign up for free voting resources at LouGarino.com

indictments, corruption and scandals. He is fighting subpoenas as well as fighting for the same donors as Bush. Great thing is that these donors are so rich, they can buy them both. Christie also has a PAC, Leadership Matters for America, and they just set up a brand new Super PAC called America Leads. PACs are the sneakiest way to funnel private money into candidate's pockets that ever existed. They must be ended or reformed severely. The Republican Party was so desperate for someone other than Mitt in 2012, they were begging Christie to run. He should have. Since then, he's been connected with scandal after scandal, and according to Fairleigh Dickerson Public Mind Poll, has a 30% approval rate in his OWN state! He took a nine-billion-dollar environmental lawsuit settlement from Exxon and somehow, negotiated it down to 225 million. No kidding. It's a small wonder his disapproval on the same poll is 55%. He might make a splash in the debates with his bully pulpit, but I don't think America wants another already proven bad leader in the White House. I know I don't.

Rafael "Ted" Cruz- Current Senator Texas- If Ted is going to make any splash, he'll need grassroots donors. While his wife is a managing director at

Goldman Sachs, Cruz will have a very hard time getting money from the Banking and Corporate giants. Corporate money tends to favor establishmentarian candidates who are disinclined to rock the boat, i.e., Jeb and Hillary. Cruz is the darling of many Tea Party groups and social conservatives drawn to his preacher like ardor. He had 10,000 people at his announcement at Liberty University, but it was mandatory attendance, and the crowd looked bored with many wearing Rand Paul T- Shirts. Cruz is an award winning debater and hopes to make the coveted debate stage to promote these skills, and hopefully get a groundswell from the far right and the TEA Party. I don't think he is going to sale beyond that narrow constituency.

Carly Fiorina- former CEO Hewlett Packard 1999-2005- A poor CEO from a decade ago just trying to up her appearance and speech fees by saying she was a presidential candidate. Twice! No one liked her the first time in 2012 so she had to come back just to make sure people still don't like her. They don't! To me, anyone who uses this process for PR is shameful, but I guess that's not all that uncommon.

Fear and Loathing: Voting in America in 2016
an Anti-Partisan Apathy to Action Approach by Lou Garino

Lindsey Graham- current Senator South Carolina- Lindsey has intestinal fortitude just by entering this race. A weak, unrecognized Senator with no money, no support and no message throws his hat into an already bloated Republican field, and certainly is showing the gull for the job. This process is not a lark, Lindsey. Please go away to your rank and file senate world and continue to keep things stalling as you have been. Ever think of selling encyclopedias?

Mike Huckabee- Preacher, Minister, former Governor Arkansas- Another long lost politician prostituting a run for the presidency of the United States for prizes and parting gifts. His parting gift in 2012 was a show on Fix News with books and trinkets to follow. Yes, you can go online for all your "I like Mike" gear. He runs solely on his moral agenda, trying to take the Republican Party to the extreme right as the last vestige of the "Moral Majority" holds on for dear life. Go back to Fox, Mike, and preach to your choir. Sell them another book and throw in some trinkets.

Bobby Jindal-Outgoing Governor of Louisiana- Jindal has a PAC of his own and being a two term Governor, he probably has a list of favors (cash) coming. Once a rapid rising Republican star, his light has faded now that the policies he put in place in Louisiana are crushing the state into huge deficits, and even bigger cuts on education and everything else. You can talk out of the side of your mouth about cutting taxes, cutting taxes, and he did cut taxes. His policies, that gave so many corporate and top end tax breaks, is putting the state in the ground. What makes it so devastating is that oil prices have dropped and so has the revenue his state receives. So here's Bobby, packing a whopping 27% approval rate in his home state. Doesn't look like he's got much mojo working at home to build from. He's probably hoping his presidential bid will help resurrect a dying political career. He is wrong. The best he can hope for is an appointment of some kind or it's off to work for the banks or be a lobbyist for a special interest group. See ya'!

George Pataki- former Governor New York- Where he gets whatever contribution crumbs he can scrape up is of no relevance. George's ship has long set sail. He'll be the last candidate to run on 911 leadership, as he was the governor of New York at the time, thank God! He had better be careful not to talk too much about 911 or people will hold him accountable, as governor at the time of the attack, that he didn't require a full, complete and honest investigation. I guess folks get used to the limelight and will do anything to get on T.V. one last time. Like an old limping athlete coming back for one last try out in Spring Training. Not feeling ya', don't let the door hit you in the ass, Pal.

Rand Paul- current Senator Kentucky- Paul definitely will not get big Corporation money, Wall Street money or any of the big money from policy buyers. Paul has a huge grass roots appeal and will raise money by building on it. He'll get the small donors, small to medium business owners and he's even using Bitcoin. I think George Washington used bitcoin for his campaign, I'll check. Rand is known for his Libertarian views and attracting younger members of the Republican Party and the TEA Party. Rand, like his father Ron Paul, is a Medical Doctor first, having practiced Ophthalmology since 1993. His first political seat is the one he has now after being elected to the U.S. Senate in 2010. I wished it was mandatory for any politician to have a "real" non-government job before being able to serve the public. You don't know squat until you've had to run your own business with your own money without being able to print it when you wanted. I think Paul has many good ideas: Eliminating the Patriot Act, Non- Interventionist, Term Limits, Balanced Budget Amendment and again TERM LIMITS, no one else even mentions it. I can't wait to see how Paul takes these issues to the Republican debates and how the candidates respond. The debates should have more people like Rand Paul.

Rick Perry- Rick is a life-long Texas politician from a wealthy family, so he'll get as much oil money as he needs- But "Perry II: The Silk Purse from a New Sow's Ear" may not play out like a Longhorn's second half comeback. Once the Bulls Out of the Barn, it's nearly impossible to get it back in. Rick came out of the gate in 2012 like a champion bull rider at the County Fair, only to get severely tossed on his intellect five seconds into the semifinal round. America is now keeping those homespun simple cowboys from Texas on a short lead. Studying world affairs over the last few years, and hiring an image consultant to pick your new eye glasses to exude a scholastic appeal, won't hide your five second ride. It certainly can't hide the bandit cowboy from Texas that rode through and pillaged the town before you. See you around, Houston Rick, I'll buy you a beer. P.S. There are "Wanted" posters up all over the world for that guy.

Marco Rubio- current Senator Florida- Marco is the young darling of the Republican Party, but is having trouble raising funds. He's second fiddle to Bush with the big Florida donors, and he has no national appeal like Ted Cruz with the Evangelical Right, or Rand Paul with the Libertarians. He's spent more time with donors than the voters, and he's had to cancel some fundraising events due to lack of response from donors. If you can't get big donors from big business to which you serve, that's strike one. If you can't or won't get your message out, and you can't get a groundswell behind you, that's strike two. It appears the TEA party is even getting cold on Marco with his money spending votes. If Marco can't get some Daddy Warbucks soon, he might find his initial surge fading, and the road could be a short road no matter your darling status. You must be trusted to fall in line if you want the big pockets, but you never know. With all candidates, the money gets behind momentum, either grass roots or corporate ties. Marco might catch fire, but I'm not seeing it.

Rick Santorum- former Senator Pennsylvania- Rick is another candidate that got voted out of his senate seat, so he figures he'll run for president. Why not? The people in Pennsylvania don't want me, how about the country? Maybe I was thinking too small! The 2012 GOP presidential pack was so weak, he finished second to Mitt Romney and took the Republican race all the whole way to the convention. His message was so powerful that, four years later, nobody even remembers his name. His money can go deep, however, with Big Oil, Big Pharma, Big Health and Cable Companies keeping him alive in 2012 until the end. His Mitt Romney Junior shtick is running shallow with today's voters. His message is even further lost with every other good, bad, and ugly Republican running for the nomination. He'll quickly be back in da 'Burgh in no time at all.

Donald Trump- CEO Trump Corporation- I guess we can say Mr. Trump is financing is own campaign when at his presidential bid announcement, he told us "keep your money, I don't need it, I'm rich." I've heard a lot from politicians, but I've never heard that. I love it! He is "The Donald" and you know what you're getting, like it or not. America is tired of rainbow speeches, then getting backstabbed with behind the door deals with no transparency. Donald shoots from the hip in front of God and everyone, and well, maybe sometimes doesn't say the exact right PC things. Well? Newsflash! ...Neither does anyone, and at least you know where he is coming from. I'm sure he'd like the power of the presidency, but he's already pretty powerful, and he doesn't need the money, the perks, or the connections. I kindly doubt the presidency could lift his ego much considering the lack of room left on that spectrum. 'Old Money' cringes at Donald; he's not in their country club or their world, and he bought all the others. Lee Iacocca, the former CEO of Chrysler and father of the Mustang, when he was at Ford, said he "could run the United States government with 100 top executives," and that's about right. I wish this field of nominees were full of CEOs and never before politicians like Donald to break the grip of the insiders. Donald could certainly make massive changes, and that's why the powers that be try so hard to marginalize him in the media. Get ready, as time goes by people are listening to his no nonsense Donaldism. He may be the only candidate that's not afraid, and that's a good place to be.

Scott Walker- Current Governor Wisconsin- He feeds from the Koch Brothers teat. Thanks to Citizens United that allows unlimited contributions to political candidates, the Koch Brothers will buy $1,000,000,000 of political favor in the 2016 election.

Fear and Loathing: Voting in America in 2016
an Anti-Partisan Apathy to Action Approach by Lou Garino

Scotty's their boy for now since he already is their biggest puppet. Make no bones, they'll back the winner of the Republicans in the general election; but for now it's Walker, and they've been backing him for a while. Two-thirds of his campaign funds for governor came from out of state, according to the Atlantic. Weird! Walker is a neo-conservative's conservative. He loves corporate welfare, trickledown economics, tax loop holes and telling women what to do with their lady parts. He's famous among the hard working people of Wisconsin for using their Union's support to get elected, and then signing the Wisconsin Right to Work Legislation, and basically gutting unions after he pledged he wouldn't. Politifact called it "a major reversal of position." A typical for Scott it seems, to say one thing, and do another. I like his face, both of them! He supports endless wars, constitutional amendment to ban gay marriage, and every other position of the neo-con agenda. I think Scott Walker should take some time to go back to graduate college, but since you helped dry up PELL Grants you'll have to take out a high interest student loan. Maybe the Koch brothers could pay the tuition for the 34 credits you still need for a sheepskin!

Sign up for free voting resources at LouGarino.com

Fear and Loathing: Voting in America in 2016
an Anti-Partisan Apathy to Action Approach by Lou Garino

Act, we must, if things are to change. Whether you are a member of the Republican, Democrat, Green, Tea, Libertarian or Independent, the time to act is now! Get to know the candidates closely. Take the time necessary to know them. Silence is consent.

Your VOTE is
Your VOICE.
Be heard.

Sign up for free voting resources at LouGarino.com

Biography

Lou Garino was born and raised in the blue collar town of Smithton, PA with hard-working parents of the greatest generation. For as long as he can remember, Lou has been fascinated with all things business. He worked in a machine shop to get through college and earned a journeyman machinist certification as well as a business degree.

Truly a serial entrepreneur, entertainer and coach, Lou has three decades of real, hardcore, business experience, performing and helping people reach their dreams. His thirst for new horizons includes over 20 years of award-winning experience in real estate as a realtor and investor, being an expert in building and rehabbing homes. Lou also a started and sold two restaurants, co-owned a General Contracting company, produced and promoted major concerts and festivals, and currently is the lead vocalist for the SubZero band and the emcee for Texas Star: The Woodlands, amateur singing competition. Lou is also the Host of Business Newsmakers Radio with Lou Garino, a weekly talk radio show on Business 1110 AM KTEK Houston TX, on the Wall Street Journal Radio Network.

Sign up for free voting resources at LouGarino.com

Fear and Loathing: Voting in America in 2016
an Anti-Partisan Apathy to Action Approach by Lou Garino

Lou brings his expert political knowledge and his Anti-Partisan views to call on Americans to take back their country by the power of the vote. Having served as a small town mayor, and further serving the community and county as a member of the Planning Board and the Tourism Borough, Lou is able to utilize his knowledge and passion of the political arena to give our country a new look, and a vision to call on Americans to get informed and to take action to dictate their future.

As part of the National Campaign for Financial Literacy in America, Lou serves as National Account Director for Banking On Kids, a program which partners neighborhood banks with local schools to open student-run banks on each campus.

Always the philanthropist, Lou has founded and is President of the Texas Chapter of Guitars Not Guns, a non-profit music program for kids that promotes music as an alternative to violence by teaching at-risk children how to play a guitar, and then giving it to them upon completion of their eight-week course. Lou has further served by distributing relief supplies all over the nation following catastrophes, and has coached hundreds of kids over a decade through youth sports with his son, Lorenzo.

Sign up for free voting resources at LouGarino.com

Fear and Loathing: Voting in America in 2016
an Anti-Partisan Apathy to Action Approach by Lou Garino

For more information, and to sign up for free voting resources and other information to build up our communities, visit lougarino.com

Sign up for free voting resources at LouGarino.com

www.ingramcontent.com/pod-product-compliance
Lightning Source LLC
Chambersburg PA
CBHW062208280526
45788CB00001B/502